British imperialism, 1750–1970

Simon C. Smith

Lecturer in International History
University of Hull

CAMBRIDGE
UNIVERSITY PRESS

PUBLISHED BY THE PRESS SYNDICATE OF THE UNIVERSITY OF CAMBRIDGE
The Pitt Building, Trumpington Street, Cambridge CB2 1RP, United Kingdom

CAMBRIDGE UNIVERSITY PRESS
The Edinburgh Building, Cambridge CB2 2RU, United Kingdom
40 West 20th Street, New York, NY 10011–4211, USA
10 Stamford Road, Oakleigh, Melbourne 3166, Australia

First published 1998

Printed in the United Kingdom at the University Press, Cambridge

Typeset in Tiepolo and Formata

A catalogue record for this book is available from the British Library

ISBN 0 521 59930 X paperback

Text design by Newton Harris

Map illustrations by Kathy Baxendale

Acknowledgements
The illustrations on pages 78, 89 and 93 are reproduced with permission of
Punch Ltd.

The cover illustration by Thomas Jones Barker shows Queen Victoria presenting
a Bible in the audience chamber at Windsor (c. 1861). It is reproduced by kind
permission of the National Portrait Gallery, London.

Contents

Contents

Introduction

The history of the British Empire has exercised a fascination, both at a popular and at an academic level, over successive generations. Although imperialism has famously been described as 'no word for scholars',[1] the very diversity of the term is one of its key attractions. The study of empire can be seen as encompassing not merely formal British territory, those areas painted red on the map, but also regions which, despite being nominally independent, were nevertheless under Britain's imperial sway. Indeed, some have identified the existence of a vast 'informal empire' which from the mid-nineteenth century grew as a function of Britain's expanding economy. Even contemporaries were aware that Britain's influence stretched far beyond the formal imperial possessions. In 1870, a former under-secretary of state at the Colonial Office observed:

> By actual possession here and there; by quasi-territorial dominion, under treaties, in other places; by great superiority of general commerce and the carrying trade everywhere, we have acquired an immense political influence in all that division of the world which lies between India and Japan.[2]

As these comments suggest, the relationship between economics and empire is central to the study of the expansion and contraction of Britain's world presence.

British attitudes towards indigenous societies are also integral to imperial history. As more and more non-Europeans were brought under imperial control, Britain was forced to confront the issues of race, religion and reform. In the first half of the nineteenth century, the liberal reforming ideas which were prevalent in metropolitan Britain began to be applied to the territories of the empire, most notably India. T. B. Macaulay's advocacy of the creation of a class of persons 'Indian in blood and colour, but English in taste, in opinions, in morals, and in intellect',[3] was widely shared. The shock of the 1857 uprising, known as the Indian Mutiny, encouraged a more circumspect attitude on the part of the British towards indigenous societies. Nevertheless, this did not spare Britain from the growing nationalist challenge. Indeed, the final phases of empire are characterised by the interaction between imperialism and nationalism.

While scholarly attention has tended to focus on the part played by Britain's imperial endeavour in shaping the extra-European world, it is also worth reflecting on the impact of empire on Britain herself. As P. J. Marshall has pointed out: 'For at least two hundred years, from the mid-eighteenth to the mid-twentieth century, empire had a powerful hold on the imaginations of many British people.'[4] This is, perhaps, one of the empire's most lasting legacies.

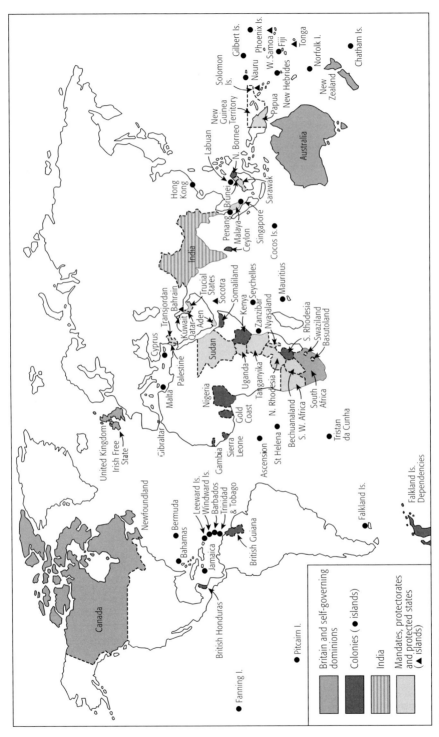

Map 1. The British Empire c. 1931

Gilbert Is.
Phoenix Is.
Nauru
W. Samoa
Tonga
Fiji
Norfolk I.
Chatham Is.
Solomon Is.
New Hebrides
New Zealand
New Guinea Territory
Papua
Australia
Labuan
N. Borneo
Brunei
Sarawak
Hong Kong
Penang
Malaya
Singapore
Ceylon
Cocos Is.
India
Mauritius
Seychelles
Socotra
Somaliland
Trucial States
Bahrain
Kuwait
Qatar
Aden
Transjordan
Cyprus
Palestine
Malta
Sudan
Kenya
Zanzibar
Nyasaland
S. Rhodesia
Swaziland
Basutoland
Uganda
Tanganyika
N. Rhodesia
Bechuanaland
S. W. Africa
South Africa
Tristan da Cunha
Nigeria
Gold Coast
Sierra Leone
Gambia
Ascension
St Helena
United Kingdom
Irish Free State
Gibraltar
Newfoundland
Bermuda
Bahamas
Jamaica
Leeward Is.
Windward Is.
Barbados
Trinidad & Tobago
British Guiana
Falkland Is.
Falkland Is. Dependencies
British Honduras
Canada
Pitcairn I.
Fanning I.

Britain and self-governing dominions

Colonies (● islands)

India

Mandates, protectorates and protected states (▲ islands)

The book is structured around ten chapters, each one dealing with a particular aspect of British imperialism. Chapters 1 and 2 examine the loss of one empire in North America and the acquisition of another in Asia in the second half of the eighteenth century. Chapter 3 analyses constitutional development in the colonies of European settlement, while Chapter 4 provides an insight into the complex debates surrounding the abolition of the slave trade and slavery in the early decades of the nineteenth century, as well as the part played by missionaries and humanitarians in shaping British attitudes towards empire. Chapters 5 and 6 survey the centre-piece of the British Empire, India, from the early nineteenth century through to independence and partition in 1947. Chapter 7 provides an overview of British imperial expansion at the height of British power in the nineteenth century, while the following chapter looks at the challenges to imperial authority presented by Ireland and South Africa. Focusing on the twentieth century, the final two chapters, 9 and 10, analyse aspects of Britain's retreat from empire. Documentary sources help to illustrate the themes and issues raised in each chapter. Detailed notes at the end of each chapter, as well as a select bibliography, guide the reader through the literature on British imperialism.

Notes and references

1 This dictum came from the pen of Keith Hancock. See Andrew Porter, *European imperialism, 1860–1914*, Basingstoke, 1994, p. 6.

2 W. David McIntyre, *The imperial frontier in the Tropics, 1865–75*, London, 1967, p. 11.

3 Ronald Hyam, *Britain's imperial century, 1815–1914*, 2nd edn, Basingstoke, 1993, p. 118.

4 P. J. Marshall, 'Imperial Britain', *Journal of Imperial and Commonwealth History*, vol. 23 (1995): 393.

1 The Seven Years War and crisis in North America

Key dates

1756–63 Seven Years War
1764 Sugar Act
1765 Stamp Act
1766 Declaratory Act
1767 Townshend Duties
1773 Tea Act
      16 December: Boston Tea Party
1774 'Intolerable' Acts
      Quebec Act
      First Continental Congress
1776 *4 July:* Declaration of Independence

Centred on North America, Britain's first empire had grown as a result of English migration rather than conquest. By the mid-eighteenth century, nevertheless, North America had become the scene of mounting Anglo-French conflict, which soon merged with a wider European and global struggle known as the Seven Years War. Although Britain emerged victorious, the long years of war had the effect of irrevocably altering her relationship with the American colonies: while British statesmen resolved to assert imperial supremacy, the colonists were equally determined to maintain and extend their freedoms. The differing, and eventually mutually exclusive, notions of imperial authority lay at the heart of the conflict which led to the Declaration of American Independence in 1776.

The nature of imperial authority

Early attempts at settlement in the late sixteenth century had foundered due to lack of metropolitan support. Chartered in 1606, the Virginia Company represented the first systematic attempt to colonise North America. Despite a hazardous infancy, Virginia prospered as a result of the commercial cultivation of tobacco. Economic dislocation, political upheaval, and religious strife in the middle decades of the seventeenth century encouraged further emigration from England to North America. By 1759, the 13 mainland colonies which later rebelled had a population of around one and a quarter million, in addition to some 340,000 Africans, mostly slaves.

Economic relations between Britain and the colonies were governed by a series of Trade and Navigation Acts, the first of which was introduced in 1651. With the central aim of maximising profits from North America, these acts restricted the carrying trade within the empire to British or colonial ships, prohibited the import into the colonies of any goods which had not first passed through England, and listed colonial commodities which could not be shipped to foreign countries. The economic system which resulted became known as mercantilism. In order to protect imperial markets for domestic industries, the home government also placed a series of restrictions on colonial manufacture. In 1699, the Wool Act forbade the export of raw wool, woollen yarn, or cloth, while the Hat Act of 1732 limited the number of apprentices a hatter could employ to two. The Iron Act of 1750 sought to stifle the growth of the colonial metalware industry by placing restrictions on further expansion. While establishing its authority over colonial trade, parliament was more circumspect when it came to taxing the colonies for revenue.

Three distinct categories of colony existed by the mid-eighteenth century: charter, proprietary and royal. Connecticut and Rhode Island, on account of their charters, enjoyed especial freedoms. In addition to fully elective legislatures, the two charter colonies chose their governors by a popular vote. With the exception of Massachusetts, where the council was elected, the other colonies, royal and proprietary, possessed similar forms of government. The governor and his council were appointed by the crown or the proprietor. Each colony also had an elected assembly which by the early eighteenth century had established the right to give assent to laws and taxes, and to initiate legislation. Despite the general acceptance of these arrangements, there existed real differences about the constitutional standing of the assemblies. On the one hand, the colonists perceived their elected legislatures as 'true parliaments which they enjoyed in virtue of their rights as Englishmen'.[1] On the other, the home government thought of them as subordinate agencies which derived their authority from the crown. In the first half of the eighteenth century, the potential for conflict was masked by the British government's relative lack of interest in the political and constitutional structure of the colonies. In these circumstances the principal rivalry was played out between the governor and the assembly.

In the battle between governor and assembly, the former found himself at a distinct disadvantage. The assembly's legislative functions made it an essential component of government in each colony. Moreover, its revenue-raising powers allowed it to refuse to vote funds until its demands were met. Further leverage was provided by the fact that in most colonies the governor's salary was dependent on an annual allocation from the assembly. The governor's freedom of action was also limited by the paucity of patronage at his disposal.

In eighteenth-century Britain, political stability was in part maintained by the government's distribution of patronage, principally in the form of appointments to offices. This practice was extended to the selection of officials in colonial administration. The home government's invasion of the governor's prerogative to appoint other officials within his colony had the effect of limiting the amount of patronage with which he could attract possible American supporters. Domestic political stability, therefore, was bought at the price of diluting British authority in the colonies.

The weak position in which many governors found themselves can be illustrated by a number of examples. Lewis Morris' governorship of New Jersey (1738–46) was characterised by legislative stalemate: in one session the only public act passed was for the destruction of crows, blackbirds, squirrels and woodpeckers in three counties. Morris' successor, Jonathan Belcher, fared little better, bitter conflict with the assembly depriving the government of tax revenues for several years. In New York, crown instructions to grant the governor a regular salary were ignored by the assembly and had to be abandoned in 1755. At the time of the outbreak of the Seven Years War, therefore, the assemblies had attained a vitality and independence which belied their theoretical subordination to imperial authority. All the time that Britain chose not to interfere in the internal structure of the colonies an uneasy peace was maintained. The prolonged struggle with the French, however, led to a more intrusive approach by Britain which set colonial rights and imperial authority on a collision course.

Mileposts along the road to imperial crisis

In 1763, British dominance of North America appeared to be complete (see Map 2). Her principal rival, France, had been defeated and vast new tracts of land were added to the empire. British territory stretched from Quebec in the north, down the Back Country of the Old Colonies between the Appalachian Mountains and the Mississippi, to the tip of Florida in the south. The pursuit of victory, however, had highlighted the weakness of metropolitan authority over the colonies.

During the conflict, colonists persistently flouted metropolitan economic regulations. By the end of the war, one customs official estimated that smuggled molasses (a sugar by-product used to produce the popular colonial drink of rum) from the French West Indies had increased by 500 per cent. Not only were such activities in contravention of the Trade and Navigation Acts, but they also provided indirect assistance to Britain's French enemies. Britain's determination to tighten imperial control in the aftermath of war was matched by an equal resolve on the part of the colonists to maintain, and even enhance, their rights. If anything the experience of war had increased the colonists' sense of self-confidence and self-reliance. Not only did they take great pride in their part in securing victory, but also the removal of the French threat made the colonists less dependent on Britain for protection. 'The Seven Years' War thus sent the postwar expectations of men on both sides of the Atlantic veering off in opposite directions.'[2]

In the course of the war Britain's national debt had more than doubled to reach the unprecedented figure of £133 million. However, the urgent need to

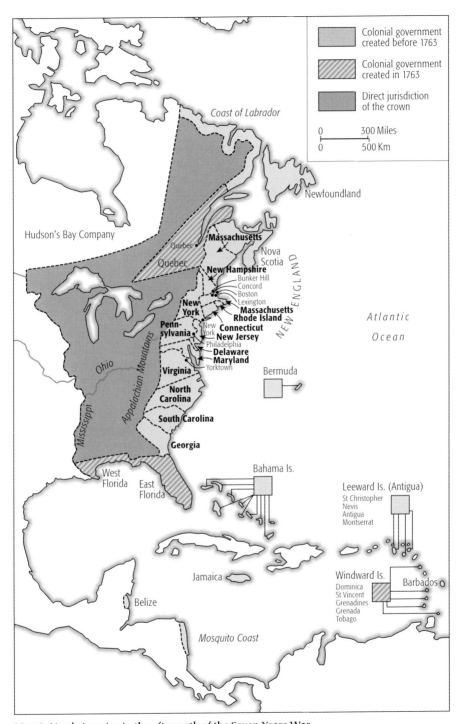

Map 2. North America in the aftermath of the Seven Years War

economise conflicted with Britain's vast new territorial commitments. In addition to about 100,000 French people living principally in Quebec, some 250,000 native Americans had been brought into the empire as a result of British victory. The necessity of maintaining a large military presence in America in order to preserve peace within the new territories was emphasised in the summer of 1763 when a great Indian rising, known as Pontiac's Conspiracy, engulfed the upper Ohio valley. Fifteen regiments were allocated to North America at an estimated annual cost of £200,000, although this figure proved to be much higher. At a time when Britain was groaning under the weight of accumulated debt, the annual interest on which was between four and five million pounds, British statesmen naturally looked to the colonies to contribute to their own defence. As an adviser to Lord Shelburne (president of the Board of Trade) remarked: 'The Provinces being now surrounded by an army, a navy, and by hostile tribes of Indians . . . it may be time (not to oppress or injure them) but to exact a due deference to the just and equitable demands of a British parliament.'[3] The task of putting such principles into practice was the responsibility of George Grenville, who became prime minister in April 1763.

A year after taking office, Grenville produced his Plantation Act, popularly known as the Sugar Act. While the existing duty on foreign molasses entering America was halved, the British government set out to enforce rigorously its collection. In 1765, Grenville produced his Stamp Act, which placed duties on newspapers and a wide range of documents. Grenville fell from office in July of that year to be replaced by the Marquis of Rockingham. Within a year Rockingham had also fallen and William Pitt, soon to be elevated to the House of Lords as the Earl of Chatham, was called upon by the king to form a new administration. For the post of chancellor of the exchequer he chose the mercurial Charles Townshend. Townshend's Revenue Act of 1767 Imposed a duty of threepence a pound on the importation of tea into the colonies. Duties were also laid on a number of manufactured products: glass, paints, lead and paper. Although the duties on the manufactured items were abandoned in 1770, that on tea was retained. Three years later, the Tea Act produced by Lord North (prime minister, 1770–82) confirmed the duty on tea.

Reviewing Britain's revenue measures in the decade from the end of the Seven Years War, Edward Countryman has described the Sugar Act, Stamp Act, Townshend Duties and Tea Act as 'mileposts along the road to imperial crisis'.[4] 'Had Parliament not passed them,' he continues, 'there certainly would have been no American Revolution.' However, the exact relationship between the financial measures taken by Britain in the decade following the Seven Years War and the loss of the American colonies is a complex question which has produced many different interpretations.[5]

The American Revolution and the historians

In the nineteenth century a Whig school of thought developed which is associated with George Bancroft in the United States and George Otto Trevelyan in Britain. To this school the Anglo-American conflict represented a struggle between tyranny and liberty, the colonies being seen as embodying freedom and progress in opposition to reactionary and illiberal royal government. By the beginning of the twentieth century, this somewhat simplistic analysis began to give way to an economic interpretation of the American Revolution. Historians such as A. M. Schlesinger and later Louis M. Hacker argued that the Revolution arose from the colonies' desire to escape the economic strait-jacket imposed upon them by the Trade and Navigation Acts. Constitutional arguments against parliamentary taxation were dismissed as a smoke-screen to cover material interest. However, the view that the causes of the American Revolution were economic in origin is open to a number of criticisms.

The economic school's portrayal of the colonies suffering under the weight of British economic restrictions is inaccurate. Staple colonial products such as tobacco and coffee enjoyed a monopoly of the home market while the New England shipbuilding industry flourished to the extent that by 1775 one third of all ships involved in the total British carrying trade came from New England yards. Britain also provided protection to colonial goods and ships abroad. Under the mercantilist system, the colonies were sufficiently prosperous to support a rapidly expanding population. In Massachusetts, the cradle of the American Revolution, economic problems were minimal; within five years of the end of the Seven Years War, the colony had established a favourable balance of trade with the mother country. Referring to mercantilism, Esmond Wright has noted that 'the system brought prosperity, assured markets and easy credits. Where it hurt, it was tacitly evaded.'[6] The arguments of the economic school are also undermined by the fact that the Declaration of American Independence of 4 July 1776 barely mentions grievances arising from the mercantilist system. Since 1945 there has been a swing away from economic interpretations of the American Revolution to an analysis of its intellectual and constitutional origins. At the forefront of this movement has been Bernard Bailyn.[7]

Bailyn examines the intellectual influences which underpinned the American reaction to British policies after 1763. While drawing inspiration from seventeenth-century heroes of liberty such as the common lawyer Sir Edward Coke, leading figures in the American Revolution were strongly influenced by writers of the eighteenth-century European Enlightenment such as John Locke, Jean Jacques Rousseau and Voltaire. In fighting for constitutional rights, leading figures in the American Revolution constantly cited classic Enlightenment texts. The profusion of newspapers and pamphlets in the colonies also facilitated the spread of Enlightenment ideas.

While Bailyn has focused primarily on American responses to British policies, I. R. Christie is keen to stress that the imperial dimension of the Revolution must be taken into account. 'Historians need to know as fully why British statesmen acted as they did as why the colonists became angry', he asserts.[8] Christie argues that Britain's decision to impose taxes on the colonies must be understood in terms of the new problems which were created in the aftermath of the Seven Years War. Vast new frontiers which the colonists alone could not defend, the growing burden of imperial defence costs, and a steep rise in the national debt since the 1750s all made the raising of revenue from the colonies a natural policy for the metropolitan government to pursue.

The interpretations of Bailyn and Christie possess much explanatory power. While Bailyn has demonstrated the intellectual conditions which made revolution possible, Christie has emphasised the intractable problem of imperial overstretch faced by Britain in the aftermath of the Seven Years War. At the heart of the Anglo-American dispute, however, lay a controversy about the nature of imperial authority.

Crisis of authority

As noted above, during the first half of the seventeenth century the colonial assemblies had evolved into legislative bodies possessing much independence and political sophistication. Indeed, the assemblies assumed, and later claimed, equality of status with the British parliament. The imperial government's revenue measures after 1763 were resented since they symbolised an attempt by parliament to assert its supremacy over the colonial assemblies. The amounts to be raised from the taxes were not the key issue. The expected annual yields from the Sugar Act and the Stamp Act were £45,000 and £60,000 respectively, although the actual sums collected were far lower. All the money raised was to be used in America. By comparison with their British counterparts, moreover, colonial taxpayers were lightly taxed. While the revenue measures were the ostensible cause of the breakdown of Anglo-American relations, it was their constitutional implications which offended the colonists. Acting on behalf of the Massachusetts Bay House of Representatives, the Boston lawyer and pamphleteer James Otis told the governor that the Sugar Act deprived 'the colonies of their most essential rights as British subjects and particularly the right of assessing their own taxes'.[9] The reaction to the Sugar Act, however, was mute by comparison with the storm of protest aroused by the Stamp Act.

In February 1765, the Treasury secretary, Thomas Whately, wrote: 'The great measure of the session is the American Stamp Act. I give it the appelation [sic] of a great measure on account of the important point it establishes, the right of parliament to lay an internal tax on the colonies.'[10] When news of the Stamp Act reached America in April it was greeted with dismay. In the Virginia House of Burgesses, a number of resolutions were passed asserting the doctrine of no taxation without representation. In October, nine colonies sent representatives to the Stamp Act Congress in New York. Only New Hampshire declined to be represented, delegates from the other three colonies being prevented from attending by their governors. In New York the Congress challenged the legality of the Stamp Act, stressing that the assemblies alone had the right to tax the colonies. Indeed, the Stamp Act was particularly hated as, unlike the Sugar Act, it was no mere adaptation of an existing piece of legislation but an innovation which sought to establish the right of the imperial parliament to impose internal taxation on the colonies.

The Stamp Act was prevented from coming into operation by intimidation of the officials who had been charged with collecting the tax. Resistance was stiffened by a group of radicals known as the 'Sons of Liberty'. Refusal to pay the tax, coupled with a resumption of taxable activities, reinforced the colonists' defiance of parliament. Economic pressure was also applied by a boycott of British goods. In the face of such hostility the new Rockingham administration realised that the Stamp Act had become untenable. In order to secure the necessary parliamentary support for its repeal, Rockingham passed the Declaratory Act in 1766, which reserved the right of parliament to legislate for the colonies 'in all cases whatsoever' (see document 1.2). Parliament's determination to put this principle into practice was demonstrated by the introduction of the Townshend Duties in 1767. These duties were especially disturbing to the colonists since the revenue raised was to be used for the purpose of making the royal officials financially independent of the assemblies. Speaking for many, the Philadelphia lawyer John Dickinson described the Townshend Duties as 'unconstitutional' and 'destructive to the liberty of these colonies'.[11] The colonists' fears seemed to be confirmed by Lord North's decision in 1770 to retain the tea duty as a mark of parliamentary supremacy. Three years later, North's Tea Act precipitated the irrevocable breakdown of Anglo-American relations.

A drop in tea sales in Britain in the early 1770s had led to the build-up of tea in the East India Company's London warehouses. In an attempt to reduce this surplus, the 1773 Act removed the duty levied in Britain on re-exported tea and permitted the East India Company to sell its tea direct to colonial buyers, thus sidestepping American importers and middlemen. With these measures in place, the Company was able to fix prices which undercut even smuggled tea. By maintaining the threepence per pound Townshend duty, the principle of parliament's right to tax the colonies was retained.

The ingenuity of the Tea Act proved to be its undoing: colonial merchants, who would clearly suffer under the new arrangements, united with radical politicians incensed by the constitutional implications of the retention of the tea duty. On 16 December, a group of colonists dressed as Mohawk Indians dumped three shiploads of East India Company tea into Boston harbour in an episode which became known as the Boston Tea Party. This open challenge to imperial authority provoked the passing in 1774 of the 'Intolerable' or Coercive Acts, which closed the port of Boston, replaced Massachusetts' elected council with a nominated one, and gave the governor enlarged powers to quarter troops. North's recourse to parliamentary legislation sharpened the lines of division. From questioning parliament's right of taxation, the colonists now began to challenge its right to legislate for the colonies. The colonists' suspicions were heightened by the passing of the Quebec Act, also in 1774, which provided for government in that province by a nominated council and no assembly. In September 1774, the First Continental Congress representing all 13 colonies save Georgia met in Philadelphia. In demanding the repeal of the 1774 Acts, the Congress implicitly challenged parliament's right to legislate for the colonies. Such demands were at variance with the prevailing notions of empire, which insisted upon due subordination to imperial authority.[12] This point was emphasised during North's speech to parliament on 20 February 1775 in which he stated:

> though I admit it is not worth while to spend the lives of his Majesty's subjects in levying a trifling tax upon them, it is certainly worth every exertion to secure their allegiance, and to enforce the supreme legislative authority of this country.[13]

In January, the cabinet had decided to send reinforcements to the governor of Massachusetts, General Gage. On 19 April, Gage's men clashed heavily with the colonial militia at Lexington and Concord. With the exception of the battle of Bunker Hill in June, little further fighting occurred for over a year. On 4 July 1776, the Second Continental Congress issued a Declaration of Independence which abjured George III, turning the revolt into a revolution. The Declaration was the spur for the outbreak of full-scale hostilities. The problems involved in supplying an army three thousand miles from the mother country, coupled with the entry of other European powers into the war, most notably France in 1778, proved Britain's undoing. The loss of Yorktown in 1781 signalled the beginning of the end for Britain. Two years later, American independence was recognised by the Peace of Versailles. The extent to which the problems of North America encouraged a 'swing to the east' in Britain's imperial direction will be the subject of the next chapter.

Document case study

1.1 Letter from Sir Francis Bernard (governor of Massachusetts) to Lord Barrington (secretary at war), 23 November 1765

It is my opinion that all the political evils in America arise from the want of ascertaining the relation between Great Britain and the American Colonies. Hence it is that ideas of that relation are formed in Britain and America, so very repugnant and contradictory to each other. In Britain the American Governments are considered as corporations empowered to make by-laws, existing only during the pleasure of parliament, who have never yet done anything to confirm their establishment and hath at any time a power to dissolve them. In America they claim . . . to be perfect States, no otherwise dependent upon Great Britain than by having the same king, which having compleat [sic] legislatures within themselves are no ways subject to that of Great Britain; which in such instances as it has heretofore exercised a legislative power over them has usurped it. In a difference so very wide who shall determine?

Source: Max Beloff (ed.), *The debate on the American Revolution, 1761–1783*, 2nd edn, London, 1960, pp. 86–87

1.2 The Declaratory Act, 1766

Whereas several houses of representatives in his Majesty's colonies and plantations in America, have of late, against law, claimed to themselves, or to the general assemblies of the same, the sole and exclusive right of imposing duties and taxes upon his

Majesty's subjects in the said colonies and plantations; and have, in pursuance of such claim, passed certain votes, resolutions, and orders, derogatory to the legislative authority of Parliament, and inconsistent with the dependency of the said colonies and plantations upon the Crown of Great Britain: may it therefore please your most excellent Majesty that it may be declared; and be it declared by the King's most excellent Majesty, and by and with the advice and consent of the Lords Spiritual and Temporal, and Commons, in this present Parliament assembled, and by the authority of the same, that the said colonies and plantations in America have been, are, and of right ought to be, subordinate unto, and dependent upon the imperial Crown and Parliament of Great Britain; and that the King's Majesty, by and with the advice and consent of the Lords Spiritual and Temporal, and Commons of Great Britain, in Parliament assembled, had, hath, and of right ought to have, full power and authority to make laws and statutes of sufficient force and validity to bind the colonies and people of America, subjects of the Crown of Great Britain, in all cases whatsoever.

Source: Merrill Jensen (ed.), *English documents vol. IX: American colonial documents to 1776*, London, 1955, pp. 695–96

1.3 The Farmer's Letters, 1767–68, Letter Four

Written by the Philadelphia lawyer John Dickinson, who published a series of letters in the colonial press after news of the Townshend Duties.

An objection, I hear, has been made against my second letter, which I would willingly clear up before I proceed. 'There is', say these objectors, 'a material difference between the Stamp Act and the late Act for laying a duty on paper, etc., that justifies the conduct of those who opposed the former, and yet are willing to submit to the latter. The duties imposed by the Stamp Act were internal taxes; but the present are external, and therefore the Parliament may have a right to impose them.'

To this I answer, with a total denial of the power of Parliament to lay upon these colonies any 'tax' whatever. This point, being so important to this, and to succeeding generations, I wish to be clearly understood.

Source: S. E. Morison (ed.), *Sources and documents illustrating the American Revolution 1764–1788 and the formation of the federal constitution*, 2nd edn, Oxford, 1929, pp. 45–46

1.4 Thomas Jefferson: a summary of the rights of British America, August 1774

Jefferson, a future president of the United States, was writing against the background of the 'Intolerable Acts'.

The true ground on which we declare these Acts void is that the British Parliament has no right to exercise Authority over us . . . Not only the Principles of Common Sense but the Common Feelings of Human Nature must be surrendered up, before his Majesty's subjects here can be persuaded to believe that they hold their political existence at the will of a British Parliament.

Source: Frederick Madden and David Fieldhouse (eds.), *The classical period of the first British Empire, 1688–1783: the foundations of a colonial system of government*, Westport, 1985, pp. 584–85

1.5 Declaration of Independence, 4 July 1776

We hold these truths to be self-evident, that all men are created equal, that they are endowed by their creator with certain unalienable Rights, that among these are Life, Liberty and the Pursuit of Happiness. That to secure these rights, Governments are instituted among Men, deriving their just powers from the consent of the governed, That whenever any Form of Government becomes destructive of these ends, it is the Right of the People to alter or to abolish it, and to institute new Government, laying its foundation on such principles and organising its powers in such forms, as to them shall seem most likely to effect their Safety and Happiness. Prudence, indeed, will dictate that Governments long established should not be changed for light and transient causes . . . But when a long train of abuses and usurpations, pursuing invariably the same Object evinces a design to reduce them under absolute Despotism, it is their right, it is their duty, to throw off such Government, and to provide new Guards for their future security. Such had been the patient sufferance of these Colonies; and such is now the necessity which constrains them to alter their Systems of Government. The history of the present King of Great Britain is a history of repeated injuries and usurpations, all having in direct object the establishment of absolute Tyranny over these States.

Source: Merrill Jensen (ed.), *English documents vol. IX: American colonial documents to 1776*, London, 1955, pp. 877–78

Document case-study questions

1 What conclusions can be drawn from 1.1 about British and American notions of authority?

2 In what ways does the argument advanced in 1.2 differ from the arguments advanced in 1.3 and 1.4?

3 Do you agree with the Declaration of Independence's contention that the royal government of Britain sought the 'establishment of absolute Tyranny' over the colonies (see 1.5)?

4 Using all the sources, offer an explanation for the American Revolution.

Notes and references

1 I. R. Christie, *Crisis of empire: Great Britain and the American Colonies, 1754–1783*, London, 1966, p. 17.

2 Jack P. Greene, 'The Seven Years' War and the American Revolution: the causal relationship reconsidered', *Journal of Imperial and Commonwealth History*, vol. 8 (1980): 100.

3 R. C. Simmons, *The American colonies: from settlement to independence*, Harlow, 1976, p. 290.

4 Edward Countryman, *The American Revolution*, London, 1991, p. 54.

5 For reviews of the historiography of the American Revolution, see I. R. Christie, 'The historians' quest for the American Revolution', in Anne Whiteman, J. S. Bromley and P. G. M. Dickson (eds.), *Statesmen, scholars, and merchants*, Oxford, 1973, pp. 181–201;

Jack P. Greene, *Interpreting early America: historiographical essays*, Charlottesville and London, 1996, pp. 311–509.

6 Esmond Wright, *Fabric of freedom, 1763–1800*, London, 1965, p. 37.

7 See Bernard Bailyn, *The ideological origins of the American Revolution*, Cambridge, Mass., 1967.

8 Christie, 'Historians' quest', p. 199.

9 Bernard Donoughue, *British politics and the American Revolution: the path to war, 1773–75*, London, 1964, p. 4.

10 Peter D. G. Thomas, *Revolution in America: Britain and the colonies, 1763–1776*, Cardiff, 1992, p. 16.

11 Thomas, *Revolution in America*, p. 70.

12 See P. J. Marshall, 'Empire and authority in the later eighteenth century', *Journal of Imperial and Commonwealth History*, vol. 15 (1987): 105–22.

13 Thomas, *Revolution in America*, p. 78.

2 Establishment of empire in Asia and the Pacific

Key dates

1757	Battle of Plassey
1764	Battle of Buxar
1765	Treaty of Allahabad
1770	James Cook surveys Botany Bay
1786	Decision to establish a penal colony at Botany Bay is taken
1788	Arrival of the first fleet at Botany Bay
1793	Cornwallis' Permanent Settlement of Bengal revenues
1799	Battle of Seringapatam
1801	Annexation of the Carnatic and part of the state of Oudh

In 1783, Britain was a vanquished and exhausted power. Not only had she lost the 13 American colonies, but also emerged from war with a national debt of £243 million. However, not all was defeat and despair. By this date, the foundations of a vast new empire in Asia had been laid. In 1786, moreover, a decision to establish a penal colony at Botany Bay was taken which would lead to the establishment of the British imperial position in Australia. The growth of British power in Asia and the Pacific has led some to identify a 'swing to the east' in Britain's imperial direction. The applicability of this concept to British expansion in the second half of the eighteenth century will form a major theme in this chapter. First, however, the relationship between trade and empire will be examined. In this context, the role of the English East India Company is of central importance.

Trade and empire

The East India Company, which received its charter from Queen Elizabeth I in 1600, had a number of distinct advantages. First, the Company was granted a monopoly on trade between England and the East. In contradiction to existing laws, furthermore, the Company was given permission to export bullion out of England to exchange for goods in eastern ports. Perhaps most importantly, its establishment as a joint-stock venture allowed the risk involved in long-distance commerce to be shared among a number of small investors.

Despite being first and foremost a trading organisation, the Company soon discovered that the use of force could be an essential precondition for successful commerce. In 1613, and again two years later, Company ships defeated Portuguese fleets near Surat. Recognising the shift in the European balance of power, the Mughal emperor, who ruled about 75 per cent of the Indian subcontinent, gave the Company official permission to operate in his dominions. As a result, a series of factories, or warehouses, were established in Indian ports. Despite suffering during the European trade depression of the 1620s and 1630s, and briefly losing its monopoly in the 1650s, the Company prospered following the restoration of royal government in England in 1660. Profits rose steadily, and between 1685 and 1689 dividends of 50 per cent were being paid to stockholders. By 1700, the Company was operating from autonomous bases at Madras, Bombay (given by Portugal to Charles II on his marriage to Catherine of Braganza in 1661) and Calcutta. As trade boomed in the first half of the eighteenth century, the Company saw scant reason for acquiring new territory. By the mid-century, however, the Company found itself increasingly drawn into territorial expansion.

In April 1756, Siraj-ud-Daula succeeded his grandfather, Alivardi Khan, to become nawab (provincial governor) of Bengal. Within a short time, the new nawab sought to assert his authority over Bengal by reducing the position of the East India Company. In pursuit of this objective, Calcutta was stormed and sacked, and £540,000 worth of goods owned by the city's European community were seized. In response, the Company sent a sizeable force from Madras to Bengal under Robert Clive. Calcutta was soon recovered and Siraj-ud-Daula's forces were defeated at the battle of Plassey on 23 June 1757. Bengal entered a period of instability which witnessed several changes of nawab. The Company's dominant position in Bengal was confirmed on 23 October 1764 when its forces defeated those of nawab Mir Kasim and his north Indian allies at the battle of Buxar. British territorial expansion in India has drawn a number of different explanations.

In the early decades of the twentieth century, a group of historians headed by H. H. Dodwell and P. E. Roberts in Britain, and Alfred Martineau in France, produced an essentially political interpretation of British expansion in India. From the 1740s, they argued, the decline of the once-dominant Mughal empire, coupled with the extension of Anglo-French rivalry to the Indian subcontinent, created the conditions for British expansion. More recently, this explanation has attracted criticism. C. A. Bayly has argued that 'The eighteenth century saw not so much the decline of the Mughal ruling élite, but its transformation and the ascent of inferior social groups to overt political power.'[1] Such groups included local princes, Hindu merchants drawn from traditional commercial castes, and landholders or *zamindars*.

In seeking to account for expansion in India, P. J. Marshall has emphasised that it is necessary to ask not only why the British were able to take territory, but also why they wished to do so.[2] Those historians who focus on Anglo-French rivalry and Mughal decline are essentially answering the first question.

In seeking to answer the second, Marshall stresses that it is important to explain the dynamism that led the British to exploit prevailing political conditions in India in the interests of taking territory.

In the eighteenth century, both the court of directors in London, which ran the East India Company, and the British government abhorred the use of force for commercial ends. In the wake of the fall of Calcutta in 1756, the directors in London stressed that 'pacifick [sic] measures' represented 'the best means of promoting the commercial interests of the Company and avoiding the heavy expences' of war.[3] As late as 1782, the House of Commons admonished that 'to pursue schemes of conquest and extent of dominion, are measures repugnant to the wish, the honour, and the policy of this nation' (see document 2.3). The expansionist dynamic, therefore, had to come from India.

As we have seen, from the Company's earliest encounters with India, force had been used to facilitate trade. In the seventeenth and eighteenth centuries, the resulting conflict rarely led to open warfare because of the relative weakness of the forces available to the Company. By the second half of the eighteenth century, the growth of British naval and military power in India allowed it to break down the barriers to trade more effectively, even to the extent of displacing local rulers, such as Siraj-ud-Daula, who sought to restrict Company activities. The Madras army by 1759 comprised two battalions of Europeans, six battalions of sepoys (Indian troops), two artillery companies, and a regiment of British regulars. Two years later, there were some 1,200 Europeans supported by 8,500 sepoys in Bengal. Within twenty years, this army had expanded to 4,000 Europeans and 26,000 sepoys. The new military forces not only facilitated expansion but also provided a strong motive for extracting fresh concessions from local rulers.

Between 1760 and 1770, the Company spent £8 million on the military in Bengal. In order to remain solvent, the Company found it necessary to use Indian revenues to meet a large part of these costs. Typically, it would reach agreements with Indian rulers to assume the defence of their territories. In return, they would agree to disband their own forces and allocate part of their revenue to pay for Company troops. Rulers who failed to maintain payments found the Company assuming control of parts of their administration. In 1760, large areas of Bengal were annexed by the Company, to pay for the army. The £600,000 which these territories yielded proved inadequate, and in 1764 a further grant of 500,000 rupees per month was secured from the nawab. A year later, the Company took complete control of the administration of Bengal revenues. A similar pattern of revenue allocations to subsidise Company forces was repeated in Oudh and the Carnatic. Summarising this process, Marshall has written: 'The road from becoming the ally of an independent ruler, to exercising a military protectorate over him, to displacing him altogether was an easy one. At each stage the needs of the army forced the Company on.'[4] In Marshall's analysis, the impetus for expansion derived not from well-laid policies emanating from London, but from the decisions of those on the ground in India. A related explanation for the growth of empire in India is given by John S. Galbraith.

Galbraith seeks to explain the dichotomy between the declared policy of non-expansion and the fact of expansion with reference to the 'turbulent frontier'.[5] This area consisted of land adjacent to, but outside, the control of imperial authority. Turbulence on this frontier, caused by rival military powers, both Indian and European, could undermine the stability of areas under British control. In consequence, Company servants saw the necessity of advancing the frontier in order to protect existing imperial territory. The primitive nature of communications afforded those in India considerable freedom of action.

Even in the early nineteenth century, up to two and a half years could elapse before a governor-general received a reply to the most pressing dispatch. Despite establishing a board of control in 1784 to oversee Company affairs, the British government found it difficult to exercise any degree of control over those on the spot in India. This was particularly true of headstrong individuals such as Lord Wellesley, who was appointed governor-general in 1798. Writing to the president of the board of control, Henry Dundas, en route to India, the new governor-general candidly admitted: 'I am aware that I cannot receive your opinions for a long time. In that interval circumstances may compel me to decide some of these important questions upon my own judgement.'[6] These words proved prophetic. The renewal of the French threat, coupled with local hostility to the British presence in India, provided Wellesley with a justification to embark on an aggressive, expansionist policy in defiance of Company instructions.

In the rulers of Mysore, first Haider Ali Khan and then Tipu Sultan, the Company was confronted by implacable and determined foes. Concerned about French intrigue in Mysore, Wellesley precipitated war with Tipu Sultan, defeating his forces at the battle of Seringapatam in 1799 and subsequently seizing part of the state. Company hegemony in southern India was completed by Wellesley's annexation of the Carnatic in 1801. The acquisitive governor-general also extended Company territory in northern India. In 1801, he offered the wazir of Oudh a stark choice of surrendering the whole of his state or making major territorial concessions to the Company.[7] The harassed wazir sensibly agreed to the second option and yet further land was added to the Company's domains. A further round of acquisitions resulted from Wellesley's wars with the Maratha states from 1803. Despite condemning Wellesley's military expenditures, the Company directors could do little to restrict the governor-general's expansionist policies. By the time of his departure from India in 1805, Wellesley had plunged the Company deep into debt. Another Company servant who embroiled his employers in new responsibilities was the victor at Plassey, Robert Clive.

In 1765, Clive returned to India as governor of Bengal. Commenting on the erosion of the power of the traditional rulers since 1757, he declared: 'We must indeed become the Nabobs [nawabs] ourselves.'[8] Clive ensured effective Company control of Bengal, Bihar and Orissa by the Treaty of Allahabad signed on 12 August 1765. Under the terms of this treaty, the Mughal emperor ceded the *diwani*, or financial administration, of these territories to the Company. Clive's confident predictions of huge profits from tax revenues were hollow since he failed to take account of the increased costs of administering and defending the new territories. Figures in London showed that the Company actually incurred a loss as a result of accepting the *diwani*. In an attempt to put the Company's finances on a firmer footing, Lord Cornwallis (governor-general, 1786–93) instituted his Permanent Settlement of Bengal land revenues in 1763. This scheme, which aimed to raise a fixed annual sum, placed responsibility for the collection of taxes on the *zamindars*.

The Company's shift from trade to administration was confirmed in 1813 when its monopoly on trade with India was revoked by the British government. By this date the foundations for British domination of the whole Indian subcontinent had been laid. The growth of British power in Asia in the second half of the eighteenth century has led some historians to identify a 'swing to the east' in Britain's imperial direction.[9] Peter Marshall, however, has refuted this assertion, arguing that 'In terms of wealth, trade, European colonists and territorial extent, the major interests of the British Empire remained transatlantic'.[10] Between the middle and the end of the eighteenth century, British exports to North America and the West Indies recorded five-fold and eight-fold increases respectively. In the same period, exports to the East Indies witnessed a more modest three-fold growth. Despite the loss of the American colonies in 1783, moreover, Britain retained extensive territorial commitments in the transatlantic world, including the basis for a huge empire in Canada. While undeniable in their scale and future importance, British acquisitions in India in the second half of the eighteenth century should be placed in the context of the general expansion of British commercial and imperial interests in this period. The extent to which the colonisation of New South Wales can be included in this process is a controversial question.

Convicts and empire

In 1786, the British government decided to establish a penal colony at Botany Bay in New South Wales. Traditionally, this decision has been attributed to the desire to rid Britain of her excess prison population. An alternative interpretation suggests that what swayed the British government were wider imperial and commercial considerations.

In 1718, transportation became a penalty for certain criminal offences. By the early 1770s, 1,000 convicts were being sent across the Atlantic every year. This practice was brought to an abrupt halt by the Declaration of American Independence in 1776. As a temporary solution to the consequent problem of prison overcrowding, felons were housed in prison hulks moored along the Thames and other rivers. Britain's failure to extinguish the American Revolution, culminating in the loss of the American colonies in 1783, necessitated the search for a more permanent solution.

In April 1770, the famous navigator James Cook had landed at Botany Bay. Nine years later, the parliamentary committee on transportation took evidence from Cook's botanist, Joseph Banks, concerning the suitability of Botany Bay as a site for transporting criminals. James Matra, who had also sailed with Cook, was another figure whose advice was sought. Matra strongly endorsed Botany Bay's claims, stressing that 'two Objects of most desirable and beautiful Union will be permanently blended: Economy to the Public, and Humanity to the Individual'.[11] John Call, who had spent his early career as a Company servant in India, was in agreement, adding that a base in New South Wales would facilitate trade. Call also advocated a secondary settlement on Norfolk Island a thousand miles east of Botany Bay for the purpose of obtaining raw materials for the manufacture of naval stores. Indeed, Norfolk Island was known to possess not merely abundant supplies of flax used to make sails, but also tall pines suitable for ships' mainmasts and spars. The committee on transportation, which was reconvened under the chairmanship of Lord Beauchamp in April 1785, interviewed Matra three times and Banks once concerning New South Wales. In a letter to the Treasury dated 18 August 1786, the home secretary, Lord Sydney, relayed the decision to adopt Botany Bay as the site for transporting criminals. Attached to this letter was a document entitled 'Heads of a Plan', which argued that

> considerable Advantage will arise from the Cultivation of the New Zealand Hemp, or Flax Plant in the New intended Settlement, the Supply of which would be of great Consequence to Us, as a Naval Power . . .
>
> It may also be proper to attend to the possibility of procuring from New Zealand any quantity of Masts and Ship Timber, for the use of our Fleets in India.[12]

The first fleet, under the command of Arthur Phillip, set sail in May 1787, reaching Botany Bay the following January.

Geoffrey Blainey argues that the prospect of acquiring naval stores, especially flax, proved the deciding factor in the British government's selection of Botany Bay. In an era when Britain's military strength and commercial vitality relied upon seapower, stresses Blainey, flax and timber were as vital as steel and oil are today. Britain's vulnerability was displayed in 1780 when the Armed Neutrality of north European powers disrupted her supplies of naval stores from Russia and the Baltic. Blainey concludes by suggesting that 'Norfolk Island was the plant nursery; Australia was to be the market garden and flax farm surrounded by gaol walls.'[13] Support for this argument has been given by Alan Frost, who emphasises that within a short time of arriving, Phillip dispatched a party to Norfolk Island with the instructions that 'you are immediately to proceed to the cultivation of the Flax Plant, which you will find growing spontaneously on the Island'.[14] Frost also argues that in the years 1784–86, the prime minister, William Pitt, concerned about French activities in the Indian and Pacific Oceans, became more and more attracted to the idea of 'using the convicts to create a naval base that would assist British shipping moving to and from the East, and increase Britain's capacity to defend her position there in any future war'.[15] The strategic and imperial interpretation of the Botany Bay decision is open to a number of criticisms, however.

First, Botany Bay was by no means the only site for a penal colony contemplated by the British government. Many other possible locations were considered and it was only after Das Voltas Bay in south-west Africa had been found to be uninhabitable that New South Wales was settled upon. Moreover, when the king announced the decision in parliament in January 1787, he simply stated: 'A plan has been formed . . . for transporting a number of convicts, in order to remove the inconvenience which arose from the crowded state of the gaols in different parts of the Kingdom.'[16] The 'Heads of a Plan' document, furthermore, is an ambiguous piece of evidence to use in support of the flax thesis: not only does it refer to New Zealand rather than Norfolk Island, but also its authorship is uncertain, raising the possibility that it might have been written by someone outside the government altogether.[17] On this second point, it is by no means certain that the views of those contemporaries who supported the colonisation of New South Wales were influential in British governing circles. The First Lord of the Admiralty, Lord Howe, for example, was sceptical about naval stores from New South Wales and added that he was not encouraged 'to hope for the return of the many advantages in commerce and war, which Mr Matra has in contemplation'.[18] It has also been suggested, although Frost denies this point, that the first fleet was lamentably ill-equipped for the production of naval stores: neither navy experts nor botanists were sent; the tools for the establishment of a flax industry were inadequate; the convicts were selected from the hulks without regard to their knowledge of flax production.[19] In the years after the foundation of the Botany Bay settlement, the government provided no effective support to the growth of an export industry in flax.[20] Indeed, to attribute the Botany Bay decision to a grand imperial design emanating from London is to exaggerate the 'policy-forming resources and enterprise of the metropolitan government'.[21] To what extent can the absence of long-range planning for New South Wales be compared with the lack of control exercised by London on the course of expansion in India in the second half of the eighteenth century?

Document case study

2.1 Robert Clive to William Pitt the elder, 7 January 1759

The great revolution that has been effected here by the success of the English arms, and the vast advantages gained to the Company by a treaty concluded in consequence thereof, have, I observe, in some measure, engaged the public attention; but much more may yet in time be done, if the Company will exert themselves in the manner the importance of their present possessions and future prospects deserves. I have represented to them in the strongest terms the expediency of sending out and keeping up constantly such a force as will enable them to embrace the first opportunity of further aggrandising themselves; and I dare pronounce, from a thorough knowledge of this country government, and of the genius of the people, acquired by two years' application and experience, that such an opportunity will soon offer . . .

. . . Now I leave you to judge, whether an income yearly of two millions sterling, with the possession of three provinces [Bengal, Bihar, and Orissa] abounding in the most valuable productions of nature and of art, be an object deserving the public attention;

and whether it be worth the nation's while to take the proper measures to secure such an acquisition – an acquisition which . . . would prove a source of immense wealth to the kingdom, and might in time be appropriated in part as a fund towards diminishing the heavy load of debt under which we at present labour.

Source: Ramsay Muir (ed.), *The making of British India, 1756–1858*, Manchester, 1915, p. 61

2.2 Letter from Robert Clive to Harry Verelst (Clive's successor as governor of Bengal), 16 January 1767

The first point in Politics which I offer to your Consideration is the Form of Government. We are sensible that since the Acquisition of the *Dewanny* [*diwani*], the Power formerly belonging to the Soubah [nawab] of these Provinces is Totally, in Fact, vested in the East India Company. Nothing remains to him but the Name and Shadow of Authority.

Source: Frederick Madden and David Fieldhouse (eds.), *Imperial reconstruction, 1763–1840: evolution of alternative systems of colonial government*, New York, 1987, pp. 157–58

2.3 Parliament's views on territorial expansion

Resolved, that this House doth agree with the Committee in the said resolution so amended, that, for the purpose of conveying entire conviction to the minds of the Native Princes, that to commence hostilities without just provocation against them, and to pursue schemes of conquest and extent of dominion, are measures repugnant to the wish, the honour, and the policy of this nation; the Parliament of Great Britain should give some signal mark of displeasure against those, in whatever degree entrusted with the charge of the East India Company's affairs, who shall appear to have wilfully adopted or countenanced a system tending to inspire a reasonable distrust of the moderation, justice, and good faith of the British nation.

Source: *Journals of the House of Commons*, vol. xxxviii (1780–82), 28 May 1782, p. 1032

2.4 Commons Select Committee

In 1773, Lord North passed his Regulating Act which sought to increase the level of control exercised by the court of directors over their employees in India. Within 10 years its effectiveness was being questioned, culminating in the India Act of 1784, which established the board of control.

(a) Observations on the state of the Company's affairs, 1783

Under the arrangement of the year 1773, that court appeared to have its authority strengthened . . .

[But] From that period the orders of the court of directors became so habitually despised by their servants abroad, and at length to be so little regarded even by themselves, that this contempt of orders forms almost the subject-matter of the voluminous reports of two of your committees.

(b) British government in India, 1783

Acts of disobedience have not only grown frequent, but systematic; and they have appeared in such instances, and are manifested in such a manner, as to amount, in the Company's servants, to little less than absolute independence.

Source: Frederick Madden and David Fieldhouse (eds.), *Imperial reconstruction, 1763–1840: evolution of alternative systems of colonial government*, New York, 1987, pp. 177–78, 178–79

2.5 Wellesley to His Excellency Vice-Admiral Rainier, 5 February 1801

In 1801, Wellesley chided a subordinate for refusing to move against the French without royal instructions.

The arduous powers vested in me by Parliament are sufficient to render my opinion in India a substitute for the occasional and unavoidable defect of precise and express commands from the sovereign authority of the British Empire.

. . . The want of his Majesty's express commands will never be received either by his Majesty or by the public as an admissible justification of the conduct of any public officer for declining to co-operate against the enemy in an attack which appears to be practicable, and which promises advantage to the general cause.

. . . if the principle which your Excellency has adopted had governed my conduct, the conquest of Mysoor would not have been achieved.

Source: Montgomery Martin (ed.), *The despatches, minutes and correspondence of the Marquess Wellesley during his administration in India*, 5 vols., London, 1836, vol. 2, p. 757

2.6 Letter from Lord Sydney to the Treasury, 18 August 1786

The several Goals [gaols] and Places for the Confinement of Felons in this Kingdom being in so crowded a State that greatest danger is to be apprehended not only from their Escape but from infectious Distempers which may hourly be expected to break out amongst them; His Majesty, desirous of preventing by every possible means the ill consequences which might happen from either of these Causes, has been pleased to signify to me His Royal Commands that Measures should immediately be pursued for sending out of this Kingdom such of the Convicts as are under Sentence or Order of Transportation.

Source: Public Record Office, London, T 1/639: 142, cited in Alan Frost, 'Botany Bay: an imperial venture of the 1780s', *English Historical Review*, vol. 100 (1985): 318

2.7 Letter from Evan Nepean (under-secretary, Home Office) to Sackville Hamilton, 24 October 1786

Besides the removal of a dreadful Banditti from this Country, many advantages are likely to be derived from this intended Settlement. Some of the Timber is reported to be fit for Naval purposes particularly Masts, which the Fleet employed occasionally in the East Indies frequently stand in need of, and which cannot be supplied with but from Europe. But above all, the cultivation of the Flax Plant seems to be the most considerable object. This Plant has been found in that Neighbourhood in the most luxuriant State, and small quantities have been brought to Europe and manufactured, and from its superior quality, it will it is hoped soon become an article of commerce from that Country.

Source: Public Record Office, London, HO 100/18: 371–72, cited in Alan Frost, *Convicts and empire: a naval question, 1776–1811*, Melbourne, 1980, pp. 133–34

Document case-study questions

1 Compare the sentiments expressed by Robert Clive in 2.1 and 2.2 with those expressed by parliament in 2.3.

2 How justified was parliament in claiming that Company servants were guilty of exercising 'little less than absolute independence' (see 2.4)?

3 In what ways can 2.5 be used to explain territorial expansion during Wellesley's period as governor-general?

4 Compare the justification for the colonisation of New South Wales in 2.6 with that in 2.7.

Notes and references

1 C. A. Bayly, *Indian society and the making of the British Empire*, Cambridge, 1988, p. 9.

2 P. J. Marshall, 'British expansion in India in the eighteenth century: a historical revision', *History*, vol. 60 (1975): 28–43.

3 Marshall, 'British expansion in India', p. 30.

4 Marshall, 'British expansion in India', p. 41.

5 John S. Galbraith, 'The "turbulent frontier" as a factor in British expansion', *Comparative Studies in Society and History*, vol. 2 (1960): 150–68.

6 Galbraith, 'The "turbulent frontier"', p. 153.

7 P. J. Marshall, 'Economic and political expansion: the case of Oudh', *Modern Asian Studies*, vol. 9 (1975): 467–68.

8 P. J. Marshall, *Bengal: the British bridgehead: eastern India, 1740–1828*, Cambridge, 1987, p. 89.

9 See Vincent T. Harlow, *The founding of the second British Empire, 1763–1793: Volume 1: Discovery and Revolution*, London, 1952.

10 Peter Marshall, 'The first and second British empires: a question of demarcation', *History*, vol. 49 (1964): 19.

11 Alan Frost, *Convicts and empire: a naval question, 1776–1811*, Melbourne, 1980, p. 16.

12 Alan Frost, 'Botany Bay: an imperial venture of the 1780s', *English Historical Review*, vol. 100 (1985): 317.

13 Geoffrey Blainey, *The tyranny of distance: how distance shaped Australia's history*, Melbourne, 1968, p. 33.

14 Frost, *Convicts and empire*, p. 150.

15 Frost, 'Botany Bay', p. 326. See also Frost, *Convicts and empire*, p. 121.

16 Mollie Gillen, 'The Botany Bay decision, 1786: convicts not empire', *English Historical Review*, vol. 97 (1982): 755.

17 D. L. Mackay argues that the 'Heads' document was written by Joseph Banks ('Direction and purpose in British imperial policy, 1783–1801', *Historical Journal*, vol. 17 (1974): 490).

18 Gillen, 'Botany Bay decision', p. 744.

19 Gillen, 'Botany Bay decision', pp. 763–65.

20 David Mackay, 'Far-flung empire: a neglected imperial outpost at Botany Bay, 1788–1801', *Journal of Imperial and Commonwealth History*, vol. 9 (1981): 138.

21 Mackay, 'Direction and purpose', p. 492.

3 Self-determination in the colonies of European settlement

Key dates

1791	Constitutional Act
1832	Great Reform Act
1837	Rebellions in Upper and Lower Canada
1839	Durham Report
1841	Union of Upper and Lower Canada
1848	Responsible government conceded to Canada
1917	Imperial War Cabinet established
1922	Chanak Crisis
1926	Balfour Report
1931	Statute of Westminster
1932	Ottawa Imperial Economic Conference
1940	Ogdensburg Agreement
1951	Pacific Security Agreement
1963	Britain's first application to join the European Economic Community is vetoed
1972	Treaty of Accession paves the way for Britain's entry into the EEC

The colonies of European settlement – Canada, Australia, New Zealand and South Africa – possessed strong cultural and economic links with Britain. From the mid-nineteenth century, Britain began to devolve power to these territories. In recognition of their political advancement, they lost their colonial status in 1907, being henceforth referred to as dominions. The strength of the cultural and economic bonds, however, ensured that they remained closely tied to Britain. The intimacy of the relationship was demonstrated between 1914 and 1918 when the dominions provided both men and money in abundance in defence of the empire. Indeed, such was the scale of their contributions that they began to demand a voice in the conduct of imperial foreign and defence policy. These demands intensified in the immediate post-war years. Responding to these pressures, Britain conceded full independence to the dominions by 1931. In the short term, this concession did not alter imperial relations, and the superficiality of the change was demonstrated by spontaneous dominion support for Britain on the outbreak of the Second World War.

The development of responsible government

Attracted by the lucrative North American fur trade, French people began settling along the St Lawrence River from the early seventeenth century. By 1660, the European population of French Canada had reached 3,000. During the Seven Years War (1756–63) Britain and France struggled for mastery of North America. Although fighting continued until 1763, the fall of Montreal to the British three years earlier effectively ended the French Empire in North America. Under the terms of the Treaty of Paris (1763), all French territory east of the Mississippi River was ceded to Britain. Having conquered French Canada, Britain was left with the task of governing a territory whose population felt no loyalty towards her.

In 1774, Britain passed the Quebec Act under which the Catholic religion and French culture of the inhabitants of the St Lawrence Valley were recognised. From 1783, however, the racial composition of Canada began to alter. Empire loyalists alienated by the independence of the 13 colonies sought refuge in Canada, most settling west of the Ottawa River. In response to this development, Britain enacted the 1791 Constitutional Act, which created a British province of Upper Canada and a French province of Lower Canada.

Perceiving that the loss of the American colonies had resulted from excessive popular control of the organs of government, the framers of the 1791 Act were keen to assert imperial authority. The constitutions of Upper and Lower Canada, therefore, mirrored British constitutional arrangements. Each province was provided with a governor, an executive council, a legislative council and an elected assembly, corresponding with the British monarch, the government, the House of Lords and the House of Commons. In keeping with British constitutional practices, where the monarch selected his or her ministers, the executive councils in the two Canadas were appointed by the governor. It did not take long for the inadequacies of this situation to be revealed. By the 1820s, the assemblies were at perpetual loggerheads with the councils. Councillors could ignore the assembly with impunity, while the assembly could not bring about change in either the personnel or policies of the councils. These problems were especially acute in Lower Canada, where the English minority dominated the councils, while the French majority dominated the assembly. Growing frustration with this situation led to a rebellion in Lower Canada in 1837. In the same year, a smaller outbreak also occurred in Upper Canada. In an attempt to resolve the problems of Canada, the Whig peer Lord Durham was dispatched to North America as governor-in-chief and high commissioner.

Durham had a reputation as a reformer, having played a key role in mustering support for parliamentary reform at the time of the Great Reform Act (1832). Durham's liberal reputation seemed to be confirmed on 28 June 1838, Queen Victoria's Coronation Day, when he ordered the release of most political prisoners in Lower Canada, exiling the rest to Bermuda. When his superiors in London disallowed these orders, Durham resigned his post, leaving Canada before the end of year. Undeterred, Durham started writing his *Report on the affairs of North America*, which was published in February 1839.

In Durham's opinion, the conflict of races was at the centre of Lower Canada's problems. 'I expected to find', he wrote, 'a contest between a government and a people: I found two nations warring in the bosom of a single state: I found a struggle, not of principles, but of races' (see document 3.1). To overcome this problem, he advocated a union of the two Canadas in which the French would be outnumbered by the English majority. In addition to racial conflict, Durham identified the constant clash between executive and assembly as a major source of political dissatisfaction in both Canadas (see document 3.2). Durham's remedy was responsible government under which local affairs would be delegated to executive councillors who could command the confidence of a majority in the assembly. Under these circumstances, the executive, or government, would be responsible to the elected assembly. Durham also addressed the question of reconciling local autonomy with imperial control. Although Britain would be obliged to defer to local opinion in domestic matters, she would retain control of imperial concerns such as the regulation of foreign and commercial relations.

Although largely neglected by contemporaries, the report came to assume great importance from the late nineteenth century. Historians, both British and Canadian, saw it as the Magna Carta of empire, providing a system of government which allowed politically mature colonies to remain within the empire. More recent historical judgement has been less favourable. First, Durham's advocacy of a legislative union was neither original nor influential. Such a union was suggested by the Lower Canada British minority as far back as 1822. In addition, the decision in 1841 to establish a legislative union owed more to the influence of the colonial secretary, Lord John Russell, than to that of Durham. There was also a marked lack of reference to the Durham Report during the debates which preceded the introduction of responsible government in Canada in 1847–48. Furthermore, the form of responsible government which was introduced differed significantly from Durham's recommendations. By contrast with Durham's emphasis on racial conflict and the need to subsume the French Canadians within an English majority, the form of responsible government conceded was one based on Anglo-French partnership. This was symbolised on 4 March 1848 when the first responsible ministry was formed by Robert Baldwin and Louis Hippolyte Lafontaine. Britain's willingness to allow Canadians to conduct their own internal affairs was underlined in 1849 when the governor, Lord Elgin, gave his assent to the controversial Rebellion Losses Bill, which provided compensation for losses suffered during the 1837 rebellion in Lower Canada.

If the granting of responsible government cannot be ascribed to the influence of the Durham Report, what did persuade the British government to make this concession? One possible explanation is that Earl Grey, who became colonial secretary in 1846, sought to foreclose possible intervention by the United States by redressing Canadian grievances. Grey may also have felt that by making timely concessions, Canada would uphold British interests in North America by becoming a counterweight to the United States. The most plausible explanation for the granting of responsible government is provided by an analysis of changes occurring in British constitutional arrangements in the 1840s.[1]

In the early 1830s, the appointment and removal of ministers was still at the monarch's discretion. The Great Reform Act of 1832 had the effect of eroding the political power of the monarch. By abolishing a number of smaller constituencies which had formerly been open to royal influence, the Act reduced the number of seats which the monarch could command at general elections to only 20 or 30.

The consequences of the Great Reform Act were not immediately apparent. In 1834, William IV dismissed the ministry of Lord Melbourne despite the fact that it enjoyed a majority in the Commons. Moreover, in the late 1830s Melbourne's unpopular second ministry was sustained in power by the confidence of Queen Victoria. In June 1841, the Conservative Party leader, Robert Peel, secured a Commons majority expressing a lack of confidence in the Melbourne adminis-tration. The principle that it was the Commons, rather than the monarch, which could choose or remove a ministry was reinforced in 1846 when Peel resigned following the loss of majority support in the lower house as a result of the Corn Laws crisis. Having achieved responsible government herself, Britain was prepared to extend this form of government to colonies which had reached sufficient political maturity. In 1856, the Australian colonies and New Zealand gained the right of responsible government. A similar concession was made to the Cape Colony in 1872. Furthermore, the national constitutions granted to the Canadian Confederation in 1867, Australia in 1901 and South Africa in 1909 all recognised the principle of responsible government. Realising that these territories were outgrowing their colonial status, Britain transferred responsibility for them to a separate dominions section within the Colonial Office in 1907. Regular contact between Britain and the dominions was also maintained by Colonial Conferences, which after 1907 were renamed Imperial Conferences. With the storm clouds gathering over Europe in the years before 1914, the dominions also began to take an active role in imperial defence.

In 1902, the Committee of Imperial Defence was formed as an advisory body on the defence of the empire. A year later, the Canadian minister of militia, Sir Frederick Borden, attended sessions of the committee while in London on other business. The right of the dominions both to seek the advice of the committee, and be represented in resulting discussions, was formalised at the 1907 Colonial Conference. Four years later, the dominion premiers were invited to a special meeting of the Committee of Imperial Defence at which the foreign secretary, Sir Edward Grey, outlined Britain's approach to the growing European crisis. Despite the increased level of consultation symbolised by this gathering, Britain still formulated the empire's foreign policy. Thus, when George V declared war on Germany in August 1914, he did so on behalf of the whole empire. The unilateral declaration did not dampen dominion enthusiasm for this imperial cause.

The dominions at war

'When the Empire is at war,' declared the Australian prime minister, Joseph Cook, 'so Australia is at war.'[2] Cook immediately placed the Australian navy under British control, and offered to provide an expeditionary force of 20,000. Canada and New Zealand also unhesitatingly pledged military support for the imperial war effort. South Africa was the only dominion which demonstrated divided loyalties. Between 1899 and 1902, the Dutch settlers, known as Boers or Afrikaners, had fought a bitter war against Britain (see Chapter 8). With memories of this conflict still fresh, an extreme Afrikaner nationalist, Colonel S. G. Maritz, led a rebellion in protest at South African involvement in the First World War. By February 1915, the rebellion had been extinguished by loyal Afrikaner troops. Although South Africa's involvement in the First World War was delayed by the Maritz rebellion, South African forces played a distinguished part in the military operations against the German colonies in Africa. In the first half of 1915, for example, 40,000 South Africans drove enemy forces from German South West Africa. Furthermore, over 2,000 white South Africans died in the process of ejecting the Germans from East Africa. Perhaps the most heroic, if futile, action involving dominion troops took place at Gallipoli.

In an attempt to knock Germany's Turkish ally out of the war, members of the Australian and New Zealand Army Corps (ANZACS), along with the British 29th division, were dispatched to Gallipoli at the entrance to the Dardanelle Straits on 25 April 1915. From their fortified positions, the Turks inflicted heavy casualties on the besiegers. By the time the order to withdraw was given at the end of the year, some 8,000 Australians and 2,600 New Zealanders had lost their lives. Despite the failure of the Gallipoli action to achieve its objectives, the bravery and resilience of the ANZACS was a source of great national pride – 25 April is still Australia and New Zealand's national day of remembrance.

The Canadians also distinguished themselves in fighting on the Western Front. Their most notable triumph came with the capture, against daunting odds, of Vimy Ridge in April 1917. Dominion contributions to the war effort came in the form not only of men but also money. Most of the financial costs of deploying men overseas, as well as other war-related investment, were met by the dominion governments. As a result, Canada's national debt rose from £67 million to a staggering £317 million. In spite of the impressive solidarity exhibited by the dominions, the stresses of war placed unprecedented strain on imperial relationships.

In the face of Britain's mounting war needs, the Australian prime minister, William Hughes, became convinced of the necessity of introducing conscription. Hughes put the matter to the Australian people in two referenda, the first in October 1916, the second in December 1917. The fact that conscription was rejected on both occasions indicates the limits of tolerance to imperial demands. In Canada conscription also became a controversial issue. When the prime minister, Robert Borden, passed the Military Service Act in August 1917, French Canadians reacted strongly, seeing the measure as an attack upon them by the

English-speaking majority. So serious was the sense of alienation that anti-conscription riots broke out in Quebec at Easter 1918. Moreover, the sacrifices which the dominions were forced to make during the war encouraged them to become more assertive in their dealings with Britain. In July 1915, for example, Borden demanded an improvement in the co-ordination of Britain's war effort before providing additional Canadian troops for the Western Front. During the Allied Economic Conference in Paris in June 1916, furthermore, Hughes emphasised that he spoke for Australian interests. The dominions also began to demand greater consultation in the conduct of the war. In response, the British prime minister, David Lloyd George, decided to establish an Imperial War Cabinet consisting of the five members of the British War Cabinet in addition to dominion premiers. Meeting for the first time on 20 March 1917, the Imperial War Cabinet convened a further 14 times over the following six weeks. The growth of dominion maturity, symbolised by these meetings, was given expression in the immediate aftermath of war.

Dominion 'independence'

At the Paris Peace Conference in 1919, the dominions secured separate representation. Moreover, they joined the League of Nations in their own right rather than as members of the British Empire. In addition, Australia, New Zealand and South Africa were granted former German colonies under League of Nations mandates. Although the dominions had thus acquired a measure of international recognition, their constitutional relationship with Britain remained unaltered. This dichotomy placed severe strains on the imperial connection.

In 1921, the South African prime minister J. C. Smuts noted: 'The national temperature of all young countries has been raised by the event of the great war' (see document 3.5). This new situation, however, was not fully appreciated by Lloyd George. In attempting to uphold the Treaty of Sèvres with defeated Turkey, he brought the empire to the verge of war in 1922 without first consulting the dominions. Mackenzie King, the Canadian premier, was especially indignant, declaring that it was for the Canadian parliament 'to decide whether or not we should participate in wars in different parts of the world'.[3] The Chanak Crisis, as it became known, not only contributed to Lloyd George's downfall, but also highlighted the need for a redefinition of imperial relations. The pressure for change initially came from Canada.

In 1923, Mackenzie King broke the diplomatic unity of empire by the separate signature of a Canadian-United States fisheries agreement. Later in the year he expressed determination to follow 'a foreign policy of our own'.[4] At the 1923 Imperial Conference, Britain recognised dominion freedom in treaty-making. This still left unresolved the question of whether the dominions would be bound by the terms of agreements signed by Britain alone. In 1924, Canada claimed it was under no obligation to sign the Treaty of Lausanne, which replaced the earlier Treaty of Sèvres, because it had not been represented at the negotiations. A year later, with the lessons of Chanak and Lausanne firmly in mind, Britain signed the Treaty of Locarno, with no expectation that the dominions would be automatically bound by its terms. As if to underscore Britain's recognition of the dominions' changing status, a separate government department was created in 1925 to deal with dominion affairs. The post-war development of Anglo-dominion relations culminated in the 1926 Imperial Conference.

Although Canada had been in the forefront of challenges to imperial authority since 1918, it was South Africa which took the lead in redefining relations with Britain at the 1926 Conference. Two years earlier, the leader of the National Party, General J. B. M. Hertzog, had come to power determined to secure recognition of South Africa's independent status. The Irish Free State, which had become a dominion in 1921, was also keen to clarify her constitutional position. Thus, a committee on inter-imperial relations was established by the 1926 Conference. This committee consisted of the premiers and principal delegates of the dominions, under the chairmanship of the former British prime minister Lord Balfour. The resulting report described the dominions as 'autonomous Communities within the British Empire, equal in status, in no way subordinate one to another in any aspect of their domestic or external affairs, though united by a common allegiance to the crown, and freely associated as members of the British Commonwealth of Nations'.[5] The report was given legal effect five years later by the Statute of Westminster.

The extent to which developments between 1926 and 1931 weakened the imperial links is a matter of debate. On the one hand, the Balfour Report and the Westminster Statute amounted to a virtual recognition by Britain of full dominion independence. Moreover, the reference to their free association with the Commonwealth implied that they could exercise the right to secede. On the other hand, it can be argued that the Balfour Report and the Westminster Statute represented attempts to preserve, rather than diminish, imperial ties. First, by making timely concessions to dominion nationalism, Britain hoped to neutralise separatist tendencies in South Africa, Canada and the Irish Free State. Moreover, Britain was safe in the knowledge that the Pacific dominions remained conspicuously loyal to the imperial connection regardless of the exact constitutional position. 'If Imperial sentiment is strong in Australia,' observed the dominions secretary L. S. Amery, following his Commonwealth tour of 1927–28, 'in New Zealand it is a passion, almost a religion.'[6] Not surprisingly, Australia and New Zealand saw little need for a redefinition of Anglo-dominion relations and did not adopt the Westminster Statute until 1942 and 1947 respectively. Britain's willingness to recognise dominion equality was also made in the confident knowledge that dominion self-interest would dictate that imperial links would be preserved.

With the possible exception of Canada, which was shielded by its close proximity to the United States, the dominions still looked to Britain for military protection. This became especially apparent as the international situation deteriorated in the 1930s. Furthermore, the dominion economies were so closely integrated with that of Britain that their economic prosperity remained bound up with the imperial connection. Indeed, the 1930 Imperial Conference has been described as resembling 'nothing so much as an interview between a bank manager and his improvident clients'.[7] The interdependence of Britain and the dominions was highlighted by the world-wide depression of the 1930s. In an attempt to stimulate Commonwealth economies, the Ottawa Imperial Economic Conference was convened in 1932. At Ottawa, Britain consented to allow free entry for dominion primary produce, in return for which she received increased imperial preferences in dominion markets. The precise impact of the Ottawa agreements on Commonwealth economies is a controversial question, but the fact remains that the 1930s witnessed a marked increase in empire trade.[8] The strength of dominion ties to Britain was demonstrated in September 1939 when all, with the exception of the Irish Free State, which chose to remain neutral, came to Britain's aid, much as they had done in August 1914. It was only the strains of a second global conflict in a little over twenty years that began to loosen the ties of empire.

The post-war Commonwealth

Following the fall of France, the over-extended Royal Navy could no longer defend Canada's coastline. In these circumstances, Canadian security was guaranteed by the United States under the Ogdensburg Agreement of August 1940. Britain's inability to provide a defensive shield for the Pacific dominions was cruelly exposed by the fall of Singapore to Japan in February 1942. In the aftermath of this imperial disaster, the dominions secretary, Clement Attlee, bluntly told the Australian prime minister: 'Your greatest support in this hour of peril must be drawn from the United States.'[9] Learning from their wartime experiences, Australia and New Zealand signed a Pacific Security Agreement with the United States in 1951. If in the post-war years the dominions began to look beyond the Commonwealth to secure their interests, so too did Britain.

   Although British statesmen continued to stress the importance of maintaining the Commonwealth link, it was increasingly recognised that Europe provided better prospects for long-term economic growth. The French veto on Britain's membership of the European Economic Community in 1963 represented only a temporary setback in the move towards closer ties with Europe. On the eve of Britain's successful application to join the EEC in 1972, the British prime minister, Edward Heath, told the House of Commons that the idea of the Commonwealth becoming 'an effective economic or political, let alone military, *bloc* has never materialised' (see document 3.6). By this time, moreover, the original conception of the Commonwealth as an association of territories of European settlement had fundamentally altered. The departure of Ireland and South Africa from the Commonwealth in 1949 and 1961 respectively, coupled with the membership of newly independent African and Asian countries, turned the Commonwealth into a multi-racial organisation. To what extent can the evolution of the post-war Commonwealth be compared with the adaptation of imperial relations in the mid-nineteenth century?

Document case study

3.1 Lord Durham's views on Anglo-French relations

I expected to find a contest between a government and a people: I found two nations warring in the bosom of a single state: I found a struggle, not of principles, but of races; and I perceived that it would be idle to attempt any amelioration of laws or institutions until we could first succeed in terminating the deadly animosity that now separates the inhabitants of Lower Canada into the hostile divisions of French and English.

Source: C. P. Lucas (ed.), *Lord Durham's report on the affairs of British North America: volume 2: text of the report*, Oxford, 1912, p. 16

3.2 Lord Durham's views on Canada's constitutional problems

The wisdom of adopting the true principle of representative government and facilitating the management of public affairs, by entrusting it to the persons who have the confidence of the representative body, has never been recognised in the government of the North American Colonies. All the officers of government were independent of the Assembly; and that body which had nothing to say to their appointment, was left to get on as it best might, with a set of public functionaries, whose paramount feeling may not unfairly be said to have been one of hostility to itself.

Source: C. P. Lucas (ed.), *Lord Durham's report on the affairs of British North America: volume 2: text of the report*, Oxford, 1912, p. 77

3.3 Lord Durham's views on responsible government

A perfect subordination, on the part of the Colony . . . is secured by the advantages which it finds in the continuance of its connexion with the Empire. It is certainly not strengthened, but greatly weakened, by a vexatious interference on the part of the Home Government, with the enactment of laws for regulating the internal concerns of the Colony, or in the selection of the persons entrusted with their execution. The colonists may not always know what laws are best for them, or which of their countrymen are the fittest for conducting their affairs; but, at least, they have a greater interest in coming to a right judgment on these points, and will take greater pains to do so than those whose welfare is very remotely and slightly affected by the good or bad legislation of these portions of the Empire.

Source: C. P. Lucas (ed.), *Lord Durham's report on the affairs of British North America: volume 2: text of the report*, Oxford, 1912, pp. 282–83

3.4 Report of the Imperial War Conference, 1917, Cd. 8566

The Imperial War Conference are of the opinion that the readjustment of the constitutional relations of the component parts of the Empire is too important and intricate a subject to be dealt with during the War . . .

They deem it their duty, however, to place on record their view that any such readjustment, while thoroughly preserving all existing powers of self-government and complete control of domestic affairs, should be based upon full recognition of the

Dominions as autonomous nations of an Imperial Commonwealth, and of India as an important portion of the same, should recognise the right of the Dominions and India to an adequate voice in foreign policy and in foreign relations, and should provide effective arrangements for continuous consultation in all important matters of common Imperial concern, and for such necessary concerted action, founded on consultation, as the several Governments may determine.

Source: R. M. Dawson, *Development of dominion status*, London, 1965, p. 175

3.5 Memorandum by General Smuts (South African prime minister) on constitutional relations, 1921

Delay in the settlement of Dominion status is fraught with grave dangers. The British Commonwealth cannot escape the atmosphere of political unsettlement and change which is affecting most other countries. The national temperature of all young countries has been raised by the event of the great war. The national sense, the unconsciousness of nationhood of the Dominions has received a great impetus from their share in the great war and from the experiences of hundreds of thousands of Dominion troops in the campaigns of the great war. While these experiences have strengthened the common bonds, they have undoubtedly deepened the Dominion sense of national separateness, of the Dominions as distinct nations in the Commonwealth and the world. And with this sense goes a feeling of legitimate pride and self respect which affect the rank and file of these young nations just as much as their political leaders. Unless Dominion status is settled soon in a way which will satisfy the legitimate aspirations of these young nations, we must look for separatist movements in the Commonwealth. Such movements already exist, notably in South Africa, but potentially in several of the other Dominions also. And the only way to deal with such movements is not to wait until they have become fully developed, and perhaps irresistible in their impetus, but to forestall them and make them unnecessary by the most generous satisfaction of the Dominion sense of nationhood and statehood. The warning against always being too late in coming to a proper settlement, which the example of Ireland gives to the whole Commonwealth, is one which we can only neglect at our peril.

Source: Public Record Office, London, CO 886/10

3.6 Extract from a speech by Edward Heath, 28 October 1971

The right hon. Gentleman [James Callaghan] described the pursuit of a United Europe as an ideal which he respected. It inspired the founders of the European Communities after the war. At the time we in Britain held back, conscious of our ties with the Commonwealth and of our relationship with the United States, both of which had been strongly reinforced by the war. We did not then see how we could fit that into the framework of European unity.

The Commonwealth has, since then, developed into an association of independent countries with now only a few island dependencies remaining. It is a unique association which we value, but the idea that it would become an effective economic or political, let alone military, *bloc* has never materialised. It has never become a reality.

Source: *Parliamentary Debates, Commons*, vol. 823, 28 October 1971, col. 2204

Document case-study questions

1 How convincing do you find Lord Durham's analysis in 3.1 and 3.2 of the causes of the Canadian rebellions?

2 Offer a critical evaluation of the remedy provided by Lord Durham in 3.3 for Canada's problems.

3 Using 3.4 and 3.5, assess the impact of the First World War on the development of dominion nationhood.

4 Do you agree with Edward Heath's contention that the idea of the Common-wealth becoming an effective economic, political and military bloc had never been realised (see 3.6)?

Notes and references

1 See John Manning Ward, *Colonial self-government: the British experience, 1759–1856*, London, 1976, pp. 172–208.

2 A. J. Stockwell, 'The war and the British Empire', in John Turner (ed.), *Britain and the First World War*, London, 1988, p. 37.

3 Robert MacGregor Dawson (ed.), *The development of dominion status, 1900–1936*, London, 1965, p. 244.

4 Philip Wigley, 'Whitehall and the 1923 Imperial Conference', *Journal of Imperial and Commonwealth History*, vol. 1 (1973): 230.

5 A. B. Keith (ed.), *Speeches and documents on the British Dominions, 1918–1931: from self-government to national sovereignty*, London, 1961 (first published 1931), p. 161.

6 Angus Ross, 'Reluctant dominion or dutiful daughter? New Zealand and the Commonwealth in the inter-war years', *Journal of Commonwealth Political Studies*, vol. 10 (1972): 28.

7 John Darwin, 'Imperialism in decline? Tendencies in British imperial policy between the wars', *Historical Journal*, vol. 23 (1980): 664.

8 P. J. Cain and A. J. Hopkins, *British imperialism: crisis and deconstruction, 1914–1990*, London, 1993, pp. 109–10.

9 John Darwin, *Britain and decolonisation: the retreat from empire in the post-war world*, Basingstoke, 1988, p. 46.

4 Humanitarianism, anti-slavery and missionary activity

Key dates

1772 Somerset case
1787 Formation of the Abolition Society
1806 Foreign Slave Trade Act
1807 Abolition of the British slave trade
1823 Formation of the Anti-Slavery Society
1828 Publication of John Philip's *Researches in South Africa*
1833 Emancipation Act
1838 Abolition of Negro apprenticeship
1840 Treaty of Waitangi
1841 Niger expedition
1856–57 Livingstone's return to Britain

The late eighteenth century was a period of renewed religious enthusiasm in Britain. Inspired by new-found confidence, Christian abolitionists attacked first the slave trade, and then the institution of slavery itself. A parallel development saw the growth of Protestant missionary societies dedicated to the conversion of the non-Christian world. The two causes, moreover, became mutually reinforcing: missionaries were sympathetic to anti-slavery, while abolitionists were sympathetic to missions. The extent to which the destruction of slavery can be attributed to their campaigns will form an important theme in this chapter. Furthermore, the role of missionaries in the expansion and maintenance of the British Empire in the nineteenth century will be analysed.

Anti-slavery

The campaigns

In the late sixteenth century, the Caribbean possessions of Spain were harried by English privateers. Despite the fame enjoyed by individuals such as Sir Francis Drake, the Spanish position in the Caribbean remained unassailable. It was not until the seventeenth century that England established a formal presence. St Kitts, Barbados, Nevis, Antigua and Montserrat were occupied between 1624 and

1632, and in 1655 Jamaica was prised from Spain's grasp. Initially tobacco production dominated, but from the 1640s Barbadian planters began to turn to sugar. The cultivation of this crop was labour-intensive, and soon free white labourers were being replaced by African slaves. At first Dutch slave traders were dominant, but by 1730 Britain had become the major slave-trading nation, exporting around 1.2 million Africans between 1690 and 1760. By the time of its abolition in 1807, the British slave trade had carried nearly 3 million slaves across the Atlantic.

The concept of owning an individual, which underpinned the practice of slavery, presented problems for the English legal system. In particular, the status of slaves in England proved a controversial question. In 1772, a slave, James Somerset, challenged the right of his master to remove him from England. In giving his verdict on this case, Lord Chief Justice Mansfield ruled in favour of Somerset. It was not until 1787, however, that a Society for Effecting the Abolition of the Slave Trade was formed (known as the Abolition Society). The next five years witnessed intense abolitionist activity orchestrated by William Wilberforce from within parliament and by Thomas Clarkson from without. Tangible results were swift in coming: in 1788 the slave trade was regulated and in 1792 a bill for the abolition of the slave trade within four years was passed by the House of Commons. However, the early successes proved short-lived. The 1792 bill was sidetracked in the House of Lords and the following year abolitionist activity began to wane. Between 1796 and 1797 British Caribbean slave territory expanded as a result of the conquest of Guiana from the Dutch and Trinidad from the Spanish. In 1799, both Houses of parliament voted for a more stringent regulation of the slave trade. From mid-1804, an upsurge in abolitionist activity culminated in the abolition of the trade in 1807. Abolitionist activity reached another peak following the revival of the French slave trade under the terms of the Anglo-French peace accord of 1814. In 1823, the Anti-Slavery Society was formed with the object of abolishing the institution of slavery itself. Ten years later an Emancipation Act was passed in parliament. In 1834, slavery was replaced by a system of apprenticeship under which former slaves were obliged to do a certain number of hours' unpaid work for their erstwhile masters. Apprenticeship also came under attack and was abolished in 1838. The dramatic events surrounding the destruction of the slave trade and slavery have produced a number of different interpretations.

In seeking to account for the successful attack on slavery, nineteenth-century historians tended to focus on the role of the small group of dedicated abolitionists who co-ordinated the various campaigns. This tradition was built upon by Sir Reginald Coupland in the early part of the following century. While recognising that the abolitionist movement had an important popular dimension, he perceived the leaders, driven by humanitarian concern, as providing the dynamic force leading to abolition. 'The British Slave Trade may be said to have been doomed', he argues, 'when [Granville] Sharp, Clarkson, Wilberforce and their little band of propagandists opened their countrymen's eyes to the actual brutalities it involved.'[1] He later adds: 'It would be hard to overstate what the movement has owed to the character of its leaders'.[2] The idealism exhibited in Coupland's work came under heavy criticism from Eric Williams.

Capitalism and slavery

Williams, a distinguished Trinidadian scholar and politician, published his controversial *Capitalism and slavery* in 1944. The central contention of this work was that slavery and the slave trade were abolished for reasons of economic logic and British self-interest. By the end of the eighteenth century, the British West Indies could no longer compete on the European market with the French Caribbean islands, especially the extremely fertile San Domingo. In order to counteract this competition, the prime minister, William Pitt, supported an international abolition of the slave trade which would ruin the still expanding foreign West Indian possessions while leaving the established British islands relatively unscathed. The destruction of San Domingo's productive capacity, following the outbreak of a slave revolution in 1791, dulled Pitt's enthusiasm for abolition. The ruination of San Domingo, however, did not herald the salvation of the British West Indies. New competitors in the form of Cuba, Mauritius and Brazil emerged to challenge the British islands. These problems were compounded by the fact that sugar production in the British West Indies was in excess of home consumption. In others words, the British islands were producing too much sugar too expensively. In an effort to restrict production, first the slave trade, then slavery, had to be destroyed: 'Overproduction in 1807 demanded abolition; overproduction in 1833 demanded emancipation.'[3] Ideological justification for the extirpation of slavery was provided by the economist and apostle of free trade Adam Smith. In his *Wealth of Nations*, first published in 1776, Smith argued that 'the work done by slaves, though it appears to cost only their maintenance, is in the end the dearest of any. A person who can acquire no property can have no other interest than to eat as much, and to labour as little as possible.'[4]

The economic interpretation of the abolition of the slave trade and slavery advanced by Williams has been criticised in a number of ways. Seymour Drescher questions the concept of West Indian decline which is central to Williams' thesis.[5] As late as 1821, for example, the British West Indies accounted for more British overseas trade, both in terms of imports and exports, than they had fifty years before. 1806 proved to be a record year for metropolitan trade with the British West Indies, reaching £13.5 million. Although a relative decline in the value of the British West Indies set in after 1815, they 'were no negligible entity even in 1833'.[6] On the eve of emancipation, the West Indies still accounted for over 12 per cent of Britain's total trade.

The capital value of Britain's Caribbean possessions increased from £50–60 million in 1775 to £80–100 million at the time of the abolition in 1807. At the end of the eighteenth century, furthermore, the number of slaves being exported in British ships, far from decreasing, was in fact growing: between 1791 and 1800 an annual average of nearly 45,000 was achieved, compared with 25,400 for the period 1771–80. Profits for the slave trade also remained high, yielding an average of a little under 10 per cent on invested capital in the years 1761–1807. Williams' overproduction theory is also open to question.

In the course of 1806, Britain's sugar markets in Europe crumbled as a result of the success of French arms. This process culminated at the end of 1806 in Napoleon's Berlin Decrees, which aimed to exclude Britain from the markets of central and western Europe. As sugar built up in British warehouses, a parliamentary committee was established to investigate possible remedies. The resulting report declared: 'there seems no ground whatever to believe that this increased quantity of sugar in hand is owing to any cause except the diminution of the demand of raw and refined sugars . . . for Foreign Markets'.[7] In the early months of 1807, when parliament was considering both the slave trade and the problems of imperial commerce, abolition was not seen as a cure for overproduction. The inadequacy of economic interpretations of abolition and emancipation necessitate an assessment of other factors, more particularly the anti-slavery campaigns in Britain.

The domestic context

Roger Anstey asserts that 'it was as a political campaign that abolition had to succeed',[8] and in consequence concentrates on events in parliament, and in particular the manœuvrings which surrounded the passing of the 1806 Foreign Slave Trade Act. This piece of legislation banned British slave merchants from supplying slaves to either conquered colonies or those still in the hands of Britain's enemies. Arguments concerning humanity were subordinated to those of national interest in time of war. This tactic eased the passage of the 1806 Act, which had the effect of abolishing at least two-thirds of Britain's entire slave trade. Having destroyed such a large part of the trade, Anstey suggests, parliament was prepared to countenance its total abolition a year later. Although 1806–07 did not mark a high-point in extra-parliamentary activity, other periods saw intense campaigning against slavery.

Each campaign was typically accompanied by a mass petition, the first of which was launched in Manchester in 1787. Despite having a population of only 50,000, this city amassed around 10,700 signatures against the slave trade. In 1814, and again in 1833, more than one in five British men above the age of 15 signed petitions against slavery. Anti-slavery also attracted more signatures than the other great issues of the day – Catholic emancipation and parliamentary reform. In the 1830s, anti-slavery reached its apogee when 4,000 petitions were sent to parliament during three separate sessions. Moreover, a national network existed to co-ordinate anti-slavery activity, which by 1833 had 1,300 associations. Vast audiences also assembled to hear leading abolitionists such as George Thompson, who claimed to have spoken to 750,000 listeners.

The impact of popular opinion on the decisions of parliament can be seen most clearly with respect to the emancipation of the slaves. During the election of 1832, abolitionists demanded pledges from parliamentary candidates to support immediate emancipation. Lists of reliables and unreliables were published and abolitionist societies threw their weight behind those candidates who supported freeing slaves. The Great Reform Act of 1832 also facilitated the abolitionists' activities. The creation of new boroughs with large electorates meant that candidates had to be more responsive to popular opinion. Moreover, the abolition of a number of smaller seats, many of which were associated with West Indian interests, also reduced the parliamentary strength of those who opposed emancipation. Further impetus was given to the campaign against slavery by the outbreak of a slave rebellion in Jamaica at the end of 1831.

Although anti-slavery attracted widespread support, the extent to which the elite leadership were manipulating the popular element is a matter of debate. David Brion Davis contends that the hegemony of a particular class or group is achieved not by force but by consent and stems from its social and intellectual prestige. Thus Davis argues that a commitment to anti-slavery 'opened new sources of moral prestige for the dominant social class'.[9] Davis also argues that the 'dominant social class' took the lead in the abolitionist movement because 'by combining the ideal of emancipation with an insistence on duty and subordination', it 'looked forward to the universal goal of compliant, loyal, and self-disciplined workers'.[10] Therefore Davis sees the attack on slavery as primarily an elite movement designed to promote narrow social and economic interests. Seymour Drescher, by contrast, rejects Davis' 'downward flowing model' in favour of an interpretation which sees the popular element as having initiative and influence of its own. In 1832, for example, William Cobbett, who had vehemently opposed anti-slavery both inside and outside parliament for thirty years, was persuaded to support emancipation after attending a working-class rally in Manchester. Indeed, Drescher is keen to stress that the movement against slavery was far wider and more popular than its usual association with religious nonconformity would suggest. For instance, although such religious denominations produced 56 per cent of the 5,000-plus anti-slavery petitions in 1833, they accounted for less than 27 per cent of the signatures.[11] Anti-slavery also proved to be a remarkably popular issue with women.[12]

Although women were initially excluded from signing petitions, they found other outlets for their opposition to slavery. First, they made financial contributions to abolition societies. In 1787–88, almost a quarter of the Manchester abolition society's income was provided by women, while Lady Johnson of Hackness near Scarborough contributed £1,000 to help ensure the election of Wilberforce to parliament in 1807. Women poets such as Hannah More and Anna Laetitia, moreover, popularised anti-slavery through their writing. Exploiting their control of household purchases, furthermore, women were at the forefront of the campaign to boycott slave-grown sugar. It was in the campaigns for slave emancipation that women had the greatest impact.

Between 1825 and 1833, at least 73 women's anti-slavery associations were active, the most important being the Female Society for Birmingham. These associations proved adept at fund-raising, using the proceeds to fund travelling anti-slavery agents, to promote education and relief work among the West Indies' black population, and to disseminate information about the inequities of slavery. In addition, by 1830 the inhibitions on female petitions had dissipated and women participated enthusiastically in this important aspect of anti-slavery campaigning (see document 4.4). Nearly a third of all signatories to anti-slavery petitions in 1833 were women. With 187,147 signatures, moreover, the national female petition of that year was the largest single anti-slavery petition ever to be presented to parliament. Reflecting in 1834 on the contribution of women to the campaign, George Thompson observed: 'Where they existed, they did everything . . . In a word they formed the cement of the whole Antislavery building.'[13] Missionaries also played a significant part in the destruction of slavery.

Missionaries, humanitarians and empire

The late eighteenth century witnessed a flowering of missionary activity and enthusiasm. Following the publication in 1792 of William Carey's *An enquiry into the obligations of Christians, to use means for the conversion of the heathens*, the Baptist Missionary Society (BMS) was formed. Three years later, the non-denominational London Missionary Society (LMS) was established. Not to be outdone, evangelical Anglicans founded their own organisation, the Church Missionary Society (CMS), in 1799. In 1813, the Wesleyan Methodist Missionary Society (WMMS) came into existence.

The often uncomfortably close relationship between planters and the Church of England in the West Indies left the field open for other missionary societies. By 1823, the Methodists had fifty missionaries and 26,000 members in the Caribbean. While smaller in scale, the LMS and BMS also established missions. In 1824, an LMS missionary, John Smith, was accused of fomenting a slave disturbance in Demerara. His death in prison led to a public outcry and further popularised the cause of anti-slavery in Britain. Missionaries persecuted in the wake of the Jamaica Rebellion of 1831 also returned home to influence opinion against slavery. Henry Whiteley's *Three months in Jamaica*, with its stories of atrocities against slaves, is said to have sold 200,000 copies in the first two weeks after publication. The BMS missionary Henry Knibb was also appalled by what he witnessed in Jamaica, writing: 'I have now reached the land of sin, disease, and death, where Satan reigns with awful power.'[14] On his return home in June 1832, Knibb worked unceasingly to rally opinion against slavery, covering 6,000 miles in the process. With the emancipation of the slaves in 1833 and the abolition of apprenticeship five years later, missionaries could concentrate on their primary task of spreading the gospel. In pursuing their calling, missionaries frequently came into contact with imperial authority. The extent to which they acted as agents of imperialism is a complex question.

Between 1856 and 1860, Britain fought the Second Opium War with China. The resulting peace treaties not only permitted European travellers to journey to the Chinese interior, but also guaranteed religious toleration for Christian converts. The close association between the political and the religious penetration of China led some Chinese intellectuals to see missionaries as agents of Western power. By the time of the Chinese Revolution in the following century, the theory that Christian missions were in essence the 'ideological arm of Western imperial aggression' had gained currency.[15] This crude characterisation masked the subtle and complex connection between missionaries and imperial power.

In the late eighteenth century the relationship between missionaries and state was typified by mutual suspicion. On the one hand, missionaries saw themselves as part of a universal community which had no need of state support. On the other, the British government feared that the activities of missionaries could destabilise the empire. In the course of the nineteenth century, however, a closer reliance developed between the two.

Living and working among indigenous people, the missionaries often possessed an unrivalled knowledge of local conditions. In Nigeria, missionaries provided the British government with geographical and strategic information about the Yoruba, Niger and Benue regions. Referring to such services provided by missionaries, E. A. Ayandele has described them as 'pathfinders of British influence'.[16] In South Africa, moreover, colonial governors frequently sought the advice of missionaries on frontier problems. On the other side of the coin, missionaries began to see the value of imperial power in promoting their activities.

In 1876, John Mackenzie of the LMS confided: 'the people who are living under English law are in a far more advantageous position as to the reception of the Gospel than when they were living in their own heathen towns surrounded by all its thralls and sanctions'.[17] With such sentiments in mind, Mackenzie formed the South African Committee in 1883 with a view to applying pressure on the home government to establish a British protectorate over Bechuanaland. The following year, a protectorate was declared with Mackenzie himself being appointed British commissioner for the territory. Ten years earlier, the WMMS had conducted a successful parliamentary campaign to persuade the government of Benjamin Disraeli to annex the Pacific island of Fiji.

In South Africa, the famous LMS missionary Dr John Philip sought metro-politan support in his attempts to protect the indigenous people of the Cape region (Khoi or 'Hottentots') from the white settler pressure. Following the publication of his *Researches in South Africa* in 1828, Philip managed to enlist the support of the leading humanitarian and abolitionist Thomas Fowell Buxton. Under pressure from Buxton, Sir George Murray, secretary of state for colonies, agreed to introduce a government measure to establish legal equality for the Hottentots. The need for such a measure was negated by the recognition of Hottentot equality by the Cape government's Fiftieth Ordinance of 1828. A concern for indigenous people also motivated missionaries in New Zealand.

Under the auspices of the chaplain of the New South Wales Settlement, Samuel Marsden, the gospel was preached for the first time on New Zealand soil on Christmas Day 1814. Soon Anglican and Wesleyan missionaries were operating in the area and by 1840 perhaps half the Maoris of the Bay of Islands had converted to Christianity. The missionaries' activities were threatened by the ideas of Edward Gibbon Wakefield, a writer on imperial affairs who advocated the 'systematic colonisation' of New Zealand by European settlers. Dandeson Coates of the CMS took the lead in attacking Wakefield's ideas. Missionary societies, moreover, began pressing the British government to intervene in New Zealand in order to protect Maori interests. The threat of large-scale European emigration following the formation of Wakefield's New Zealand Company gave greater urgency to missionary appeals. Wakefield's dispatch of a ship in May 1839 to purchase land and prepare a site for the first settlement precipitated the British government's decision to act. William Hobson was sent to New Zealand as lieutenant-governor with instructions to negotiate with the Maoris for the recognition of Queen Victoria's sovereign authority over 'the whole or any parts of those islands which they may be willing to place under Her Majesty's dominion'.[18]

The permanent under-secretary at the Colonial Office, James Stephen, himself a member of the CMS committee, was concerned about the humanitarian aspect of British policy towards New Zealand. Referring to the Maoris, he wrote: 'they must be carefully defended in the observance of their own customs so far as these are compatible with the universal maxims of humanity and morals'.[19] On 6 February 1840, Hobson signed the Treaty of Waitangi with around fifty Maori chiefs under which they ceded sovereignty to Queen Victoria. In return, the Maoris were guaranteed in the possession of their lands and other property. In the face of land-hungry settlers, however, the treaty proved an inadequate instrument for the protection of Maori interests. Maori frustration culminated in the Anglo-Maori wars of the 1860s. The tendency for harsh reality to impinge upon humanitarian idealism can also be observed with respect to Thomas Fowell Buxton's ill-fated Niger expedition.

Buxton had been at the forefront of attempts to protect non-European peoples, and in 1837 he secured the establishment of a parliamentary committee on Aborigines. By the late 1830s, he had become convinced that only by fostering legitimate trade could slavery in Africa be eradicated. In consequence, he advocated the dispatch of ships up the Niger River to promote lawful trade among the tribes along its banks. Buxton's ideas received the backing of the British government, and the Niger expedition set sail on 12 May 1841. Soon after reaching Africa, however, fever broke out and the expedition was forced to beat an ignominious retreat. This failure had a sobering effect and by the 1850s missionary enthusiasm was on the wane. It was the fame of David Livingstone which promoted a missionary revival.

Livingstone, an LMS missionary, travelled extensively through central Africa in the 1840s and 1850s. On his return to Britain in 1856–57, he set about promoting the idea that Christianity and commerce were mutually reinforcing concepts which would bring civilisation to Africa. 'Those two pioneers of civilisation – Christianity and commerce – should ever be inseparable', he stressed.[20] Soon Christianity and commerce became a popular mid-nineteenth-century slogan (see document 4.7). By the end of the century, nevertheless, the link between the two began to be questioned. Empirical evidence demonstrated that Christianity and commerce had failed to support one another. In response, missionaries put less emphasis on their westernising role and increasingly favoured acceptance of cultural diversity and non-European ways (see document 4.8). At the forefront of this movement were the CMS missionary G. W. Brooke and his associate John Alfred Robinson. 'We carefully avoid praising civilisation or civilised powers to the heathen', they wrote in 1891.[21] In a similar vein, Chauncy Maples of the Universities Mission to Central Africa stressed: 'the European missionary must become an African to win Africans. He must, so far as is consistent with his Christian principles, assimilate himself to them.'[22] Brooke took this to extremes, wearing local dress and living on native food.

As this case suggests, missionaries tended to gain acceptance only on the basis of compromise and negotiation. Indigenous peoples also demonstrated a capacity to absorb missionary influences selectively, according to their own local needs and interests. This was particularly evident in the case of missionary-sponsored education and work with vernacular languages, both of which were used by local people to sharpen awareness of, and pride in, their own culture and history. Drawing wider lessons from such examples, Andrew Porter has observed that missions were 'amongst the weakest agents of "cultural imperialism"'.[23] By the early years of the twentieth century, furthermore, the division between missionaries and government began to widen. On the one hand, the firm establishment of colonial regimes by this date made the missionaries less important to the colonial rulers. On the other, missionaries increasingly resented the colonial power's imposition of restrictions on their activities. To what extent can the mutual suspicion which characterised missionary–imperial relations at the end of the eighteenth century be compared with those of the early twentieth?

Document case study

4.1 Golbéry's travels in Africa

In 1783, France regained Senegal, which she had lost at the conclusion of the Seven Years War. Silvain Meinard Golbéry went out to Africa in 1785 to assist De Boufflers, the governor of Senegal, in making a study of British slave-trading methods.

During my stay in Africa, I pursued with great application, the study of this part of the world; all the accounts that I collected, convinced me that the services of the slave-trade were far from being on the decline; and I ventured to assert in a notice relative to the Western part of Africa . . . that this Continent is capable of supporting far more numerous exportations, without its population experiencing any sensible effect.

Source: Elizabeth Donnan, *Documents illustrative of the history of the slave trade to America: volume 2: the eighteenth century*, Washington, 1931, p. 567

4.2 Petition of West Indian planters, West Indian merchants and others residing in the City of Bristol to the House of Commons, 12 May 1789

Setting forth, that the Petitioners learn with serious Alarm that, on the proposed Investigation in the Committee of the House of Commons of the Petitions against the Slave Trade, a Motion will be made for its entire Abolition, on which Trade, the

Petitioners conceive, the Welfare and Prosperity, if not the actual Existence of the West India Islands depend.

Source: Elizabeth Donnan, *Documents illustrative of the history of the slave trade to America: volume 2: the eighteenth century*, Washington, 1931, pp. 602–03

4.3 Wilberforce's views on humanity versus profit

But against all, which justice and humanity could bring forward against the Slave trade, it was still to be urged, that the continuance of it was necessary to the existence of our West Indian colonies . . .

. . . For my own part I hesitate not to say that, let the apparent temptation of profit be what it may, it never can be the real interest of any nation to be unjust and inhuman.

Source: William Wilberforce, *A letter on the abolition of the slave trade*, London, 1807, pp. 103–04

4.4 Letter from Ann Gilbert to Mary Ann Rawson, 10 May 1833

Ann Gilbert and Mary Ann Rawson, both anti-slavery activists, threw themselves enthusiastically into the task of gathering signatures.

On very short notice we had petitions for signing in all the Chapels last Sabbath day, and by a vigorous canvass of only 18 hours . . . we succeeded in obtaining fifteen thousand signatures – The Gentlemen, who had been doing something of the same kind, as they fancied, for the last week or two, have, in consequence put on double spurs, but at present they are ten thousand in the rear of their truly better halves.

Source: Clare Midgley, *Women against slavery: the British campaigns, 1780–1870*, London, 1992, p. 69

4.5 Fowell Buxton and the destruction of the slave trade

What we want is, to supplant the Slave Trade by another trade, which shall be more lucrative. We cannot expect that savage nations will be greatly influenced by the promise of prospective advantage. The rise of legitimate trade ought, if we are to carry the goodwill of the natives along with us, to follow as close as possible upon the downfall of the trade in man: there ought to be an immediate substitute for the gains which are to cease.

Source: Thomas Fowell Buxton, *The African slave trade and its remedy*, London, 1968 (first published 1839–40), p. 359

4.6 Letter from David Livingstone to Arthur Tidman (foreign secretary of the LMS), 8 November 1853

There are many and very large tribes in the direction in which I go. All are sitting in darkness and the shadow of death. I hope God will in mercy permit me to establish the gospel somewhere in this region, and that I may live to see the double influence of the spirit of commerce and Christianity employed to stay the bitter fountain of Africa misery.

Source: I. Schapera, *Livingstone's missionary correspondence, 1841–1856*, London, 1961, pp. 257–58

4.7 Speech by Samuel Wilberforce, 25 May 1860

Samuel Wilberforce, son of William, was an Anglican bishop, first for Oxford, and subsequently for Winchester.

'What,' some simple-minded man might say, 'is the connection between the Gospel and commerce?' There is a great connection between them. In the first place, there is little hope of promoting commerce in Africa, unless Christianity is planted in it; and, in the next place, there is very little ground for hoping that Christianity will be able to make its proper way unless we can establish a lawful commerce in the country.

Source: Andrew Porter, '"Commerce and Christianity": the rise and fall of a nineteenth-century missionary slogan', *Historical Journal*, vol. 28 (1985): 597

4.8 Speech by Charles Alan Smythies to the Church Congress in 1892

With regard to the way in which we think it right to teach our natives, our desire is to distinguish very clearly between Christianising and Europeanising. It is not our wish to make the Africans bad caricatures of the Englishmen. What we want is to Christianise them in their own civil and political conditions; to help them to develop a Christian civilisation suited to their own climate and their own conditions. For instance, we do not allow any European clothing; it is not our business to encourage the trade in boots by spoiling the feet of the Africans for their own climate . . .

. . . It is said sometimes, 'Why do you not try to teach more trades?' Well, you must remember that if we teach the natives trades which are of no use in the particular country in which they live it will only end in the Mission afterwards, instead of making them independent and letting them get their living for themselves, having to find them work and keeping them always in a dependent position.

Source: Gertrude Ward, *The life of Charles Alan Smythies, Bishop of the Universities' Mission to Central Africa*, London, 1898, pp. 190, 191

4.9 Undated quotation from Sir Harry Johnston, British commissioner in Nyasaland, 1891–95

The ease with which the white man has implanted himself in Africa, as governor, exploiter and teacher, is due more to the work of missionary societies than the use of machine guns . . . But for the Christian missionary societies few of the modern Protectorates or Colonies could have been founded or maintained.

Source: E. A. Ayandele, *The missionary impact on modern Nigeria, 1842–1914*, London, 1966, p. 28

Document case-study questions

1 What do 4.1, 4.2 and 4.3 tell us about the profitability of the slave trade?

2 What conclusions can you draw from 4.4 about the role of women in the anti-slavery campaigns?

3 How convincing do you find Thomas Fowell Buxton's prescription for the destruction of the slave trade in 4.5?

4 Compare the sentiments expressed in 4.6 and 4.7 with those in 4.8.

5 With what justification could Sir Harry Johnston claim in 4.9 that 'But for the Christian missionary societies few of the modern Protectorates or Colonies could have been founded or maintained'?

Notes and references

1 Reginald Coupland, *The British anti-slavery movement*, London, 1964 (first published 1933), p. 111.

2 Coupland, *The British anti-slavery movement*, p. 250.

3 Eric Williams, *Capitalism and slavery*, London, 1964 (first published 1944), p. 152.

4 Williams, *Capitalism and slavery*, p. 6.

5 Seymour Drescher, *Econocide: British slavery in the era of abolition*, Pittsburgh, 1977.

6 Seymour Drescher, 'Public opinion and the destruction of British colonial slavery', in James Walvin (ed.), *Slavery and British society, 1776–1846*, London, 1982, p. 42.

7 Drescher, *Econocide*, p. 131.

8 Roger Anstey, *The Atlantic slave trade and British abolition, 1760–1810*, New Jersey, 1975, p. 407.

9 David Brion Davis, *The problem of slavery in the age of revolution, 1779–1823*, Ithaca, 1975, pp. 384–85.

10 Davis, *The problem of slavery*, pp. 467, 385.

11 Drescher, 'Public opinion', p. 36.

12 See Clare Midgley, *Women against slavery: the British campaigns, 1780–1870*, London, 1992.

13 Midgley, *Women against slavery*, p. 44.

14 C. Duncan Rice, 'The missionary context of the British anti-slavery movement', in James Walvin (ed.), *Slavery and British society, 1776–1846*, London, 1982, p. 160.

15 Brian Stanley, *The Bible and the flag: Protestant missions and British imperialism in the nineteenth and twentieth centuries*, Leicester, 1990, p. 15.

16 E. A. Ayandele, *The missionary impact on modern Nigeria, 1842–1914*, London, 1966, p. 29.

17 Anthony J. Dachs, 'Missionary imperialism – the case of Bechuanaland', *Journal of African History*, vol. 13 (1972): 650.

18 Keith Sinclair, *A history of New Zealand*, Harmondsworth, 1959, p. 66.

19 Sarah Searight, 'The Treaty of Waitangi, 1840', *History Today*, vol. 22 (1972): 117.

20 Andrew Porter, '"Commerce and Christianity": the rise and fall of a nineteenth-century missionary slogan', *Historical Journal*, vol. 28 (1985): 598.

21 Adrian Hastings, *The church in Africa, 1450–1950*, Oxford, 1994, p. 290.

22 Andrew Porter, 'Empires in the mind', in P. J. Marshall (ed.), *The Cambridge illustrated history of the British Empire*, Cambridge, 1996, p. 205.

23 Andrew Porter, '"Cultural imperialism" and Protestant missionary enterprise, 1780–1914', *Journal of Imperial and Commonwealth History*, vol. 25 (1997): 388.

5 Rule and response in nineteenth-century India

Key dates

1818 Publication of James Mill's *History of British India*
1828–35 Governor-generalship of Lord William Bentinck
1835 T. B. Macaulay's Minute on Education
1849 Annexation of the Punjab
1856 Annexation of Oudh
1857 Outbreak of the Indian Mutiny
1858 Abolition of the East India Company
1861 Indian Councils Act
1882 Resolution on Local Self-government
1885 Formation of the Indian National Congress
1906 Formation of the Muslim League
1909 Morley–Minto Reforms

The relationship between rulers and ruled forms the core of this chapter. In the period between the revocation of the East India Company's trading monopoly in 1813 and the revolt of 1857–58, Britain intervened ever more intrusively in Indian society. After 1858, despite recognising the folly of seeking to refashion India in her own image, Britain exploited Indian resources as never before. Partly in reaction to the intrusiveness of the British presence, nationalist groupings began to form. Weak at first, they nevertheless laid the foundations for the nationalist challenge to British rule in the twentieth century. Even at this early stage the religious divide between Hindus and Muslims, which would eventually lead to the partition of India, was evident.

Reform and revolt

The approach of eighteenth-century Company servants, such as Warren Hastings (governor-general, 1774–85), to India has been characterised as 'orientalist'. Indeed, they demonstrated a willingness to respect and work through existing Indian institutions. Direct contacts between the Company and indigenous people were kept to a minimum. By the early decades of the nineteenth century, however, such pragmatism was beginning to give way to the reforming ideas of liberals, evangelicals and, especially, utilitarians.

Utilitarian philosophy, associated particularly with the early-nineteenth-century reformer Jeremy Bentham, advocated the reinvigoration of society and the liberation of individual potential through the provision of good government and sound laws. Adherents of Bentham, such as James Mill, applied his ideas to India in anticipation of effecting a transformation of Indian society.

Mill, a prominent administrator at the East India Company's headquarters in London, published his *History of British India* in 1818. After condemning indigenous forms of government, Mill proceeded to champion the cause of reform: '[T]he most effectual step which can be taken by any government to diminish the vices of the people is to take away from the laws every imperfection.'[1] Bentham and Mill, having provided ideological justification for reform in India, left it to others to realise their ideas.

Figures such as Thomas Munro (governor of Madras, 1820–27) and Mountstuart Elphinstone (governor of Bombay, 1819–27) reflected the changing attitudes towards India. While accepting that they could not do everything at once, they advocated the measured introduction of liberal reforms and Western learning. 'Liberal treatment', asserted Munro, 'has always been found the most effectual way of elevating the character of any people, and we may be sure that it will produce a similar effect on that of the people of India.'[2] During the governor-generalship of Lord William Bentinck (1828–35), there was a marked increase in the pace of change.

On the eve of his departure for India, Bentinck was reputed to have told James Mill: 'I am going to British India, but I shall not be Governor-General. It is you that will be Governor-General.'[3] Indeed, in his enthusiasm for reform Bentinck showed himself to be a disciple of Mill. During his period of office, Bentinck suppressed a number of traditional Indian customs, most notably *sati*, the practice of burning Hindu widows on their husbands' funeral pyres, and *thugee*, a form of ritualised murder. Bentinck was also keen to introduce Western technology into India. 'I look to steam navigation as the great engine of working this moral improvement', he wrote in 1834.[4] Bentinck's zeal for reform was matched by the legal member of the Supreme Council of India, Thomas Babington Macaulay.

In 1833, Macaulay had emphasised: 'We are free, we are civilised, to little purpose, if we grudge to any portion of the human race an equal measure of freedom and civilisation.'[5] Following his arrival in India a year later, Macaulay set about drafting a new penal code on Utilitarian principles. In 1835, moreover, he produced his famous Minute on Education in which he argued passionately for Western as opposed to Oriental education in India. Western education, insisted Macaulay, would create a class of Indians 'English in taste, in opinions, in morals and in intellect'.[6] Bentinck, who had previously described education as 'my panacea for the regeneration of India', was strongly influenced by Macaulay's arguments, declaring that the 'great object' of British rule in India was to be the 'promotion of European literature and science'.[7] It was also decided that English

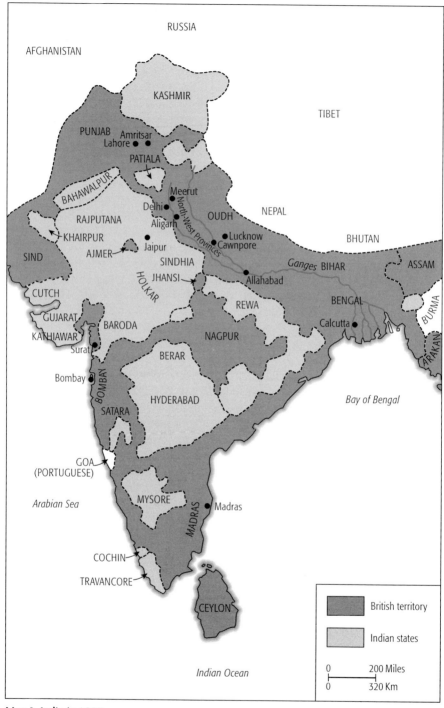

Map 3. India in 1857

was to be the language of instruction in schools. Further reforms were enacted by Lord Dalhousie (governor-general, 1848–56).

Dalhousie was a man inspired by a vision of a reformed, Westernised India. In 1850, he allowed Christian converts to inherit ancestral property, thus removing a major impediment to the spread of Christianity in India. Six years later, he permitted Hindu widows to remarry. Dalhousie was also an aggressive empire-builder in the mould of Lord Wellesley (see p. 19). In a candid moment, he admitted to subscribing to Wellesley's maxim that 'an insult offered to the British flag at the mouth of the Ganges should be resented as promptly and fully as an insult offered at the mouth of the Thames'.[8] Acting on his own authority, Dalhousie annexed the Punjab in 1849. A number of Indian states, including Nagpur, Satara and Jhansi (see Map 3), 'lapsed' to the British after the rulers had died without natural heirs. In 1856, the acquisitive governor-general annexed what remained of the independent state of Oudh on the grounds of persistent misgovernment. Shortly before his departure from India, Dalhousie expressed the hope that 'in all time to come . . . reports from the Presidencies and provinces under our rule may form, in each successive year, a happy record of peace, prosperity and progress'.[9] In a little over a year, however, much of northern India was engulfed by rebellion against British rule.

On 10 May 1857, sepoys (Indian troops) from the military station at Meerut mutinied and marched to Delhi just 40 miles away. Mutiny soon infected the bulk of the 136,000-strong Bengal army. With only 24,000 European troops, many of whom were stationed in the recently annexed Punjab, the British were powerless to prevent the mutineers taking most of the major military stations in Oudh and the North-West Provinces. Referring to the collapse of British authority in the former, a senior Indian civil servant observed: 'the fabric of civil government fell to pieces like a house of cards'.[10] However, Dalhousie's successor, Lord Canning, began assembling a sizeable force at Calcutta, and, reinforced from Britain, began restoring British control. Delhi was retaken on 21 September 1857, but it was not until the end of the following year that revolt was finally extinguished in Oudh.

The causes of the Indian uprising have produced a number of different interpretations. At an official level, the British were keen to convince themselves that it represented a limited mutiny of troops. This attitude was typified by the former secretary to the government of the North-West Provinces, William Muir, who argued that 'the character of the affair is that of a Military mutiny – a struggle between the Government and its Soldiers, not between the Government and the People'.[11] Certainly the Bengal sepoys harboured grievances about new terms of service, which included serving far beyond their home region, even overseas, with no increase in pay. Service overseas was especially galling for high-caste Hindus, who saw sea travel as polluting. Sepoy concerns reached a climax in early 1857 with the introduction of new rifles, the cartridges of which were rumoured to be greased with pork and beef fat, contaminating to Muslims and Hindus respectively. Opposition politicians at home such as Benjamin Disraeli were unconvinced by the military mutiny theory. 'The decline and fall of

Empires are not affairs of greased cartridges', he stated in the House of Commons.[12] Another contemporary who sought to examine the deeper causes of the uprising was Karl Marx.

Marx, who was working as a London correspondent for the *New York Daily Tribune* at the time of the mutiny, sought to explain events with reference to British economic exploitation of India. Marx referred to the 'British intruder who broke up the Indian hand-loom and destroyed the spinning wheel'.[13] It can be suggested, nevertheless, that Marx seriously exaggerated the extent of British economic penetration into India by the mid-nineteenth century. First, the increase in British exports, particularly cotton goods, should be placed in the context of the vast size of the Indian market. British goods, furthermore, did not always compete directly with Indian production. Indeed, local producers remained dominant at a village level. Yarn exports from Britain, moreover, may have actually stimulated the local production of cotton goods. An essentially political explanation for the 1857 rising was given by V. D. Savarkar at the beginning of the twentieth century.

First published in 1909, Savarkar's *The Indian War of Independence of 1857* characterised the events of that year as a national war of liberation against the British. While the limited geographical extent of the revolt, coupled with its lack of central purpose, militates against this argument, others have attempted to emphasise the civilian dimension to the disturbances. 'The sepoy uprising', argues T. R. Metcalf, 'was in fact little more than the spark which touched off a smouldering mass of combustible material.'[14] In particular, he focuses on the plight of established landed families who, in order to meet harsh British revenue assessments, were forced to borrow from urban moneylenders. The moneylenders in turn could use the courts to take over traditional landed property as payment for accumulated debts. Metcalf also places emphasis on the displacement of *taluqdars*, a group of magnates peculiar to Oudh and the North-West Provinces, as a result of British alterations to the pattern of land-holding. While *taluqdar* resentment undoubtedly played a part in this group's participation in the mutiny, it is difficult to establish a precise link between British land revenue policy and a propensity to rebel.

Eric Stokes has stressed that there was no direct proportional relationship between rural indebtedness and revolt. Analysing the Saharanpur district of the North-West Provinces' Meerut division, Stokes demonstrates that violence occurred principally in the southern *parganas* (revenue districts), where mortgage and moneylender ownership were below the average.[15] Moreover, Stokes shows that where non-agricultural classes made appreciable territorial gains, their acquisitions were far lower than the overall rate of land transfer. In other words, a large proportion of land transfers represented a redistribution of property within the traditional elite.[16] Nevertheless, where a great landed figure chose to throw in his lot with the mutineers, the peasants in his area tended to follow him into revolt. As Stokes has noted: 'Rural revolt in 1857 was essentially elitist in character.'[17]

The extent to which the uprising can be attributed to the reforms of the previous decades is a complex question. Certainly the lack of sympathy with local traditions which underpinned much reforming endeavour caused offence among certain sections of Indian society. Nevertheless, it would be dangerous to exaggerate the impact of British reforms. Macaulay's penal code was not applied to India until after 1857, and then only with revisions. Moreover, although Macaulay had won the ideological debate about the direction of educational policy, his proposals were designed to educate the few, not the many, and were never properly implemented. The reform era was also punctuated by periods of conservatism, most notably during the governor-generalship of Lord Ellenborough (1842–44). While opinions differ about the impact of reforms on Indian society, there is little doubt that the shock of the events of 1857 jolted Britain into reassessing her approach to India. As Charles Raikes, an officer in the North-West Provinces, emphasised: 'The fatal error of attempting to force the policy of Europe on the people of Asia . . . must be corrected for the future, as it has been atoned for in the past.'[18]

From Company to British raj

In 1858, the East India Company was abolished by parliament. A secretary of state for India in London inherited the functions of the court of directors and the board of control, while a crown-appointed viceroy headed the government in India. Another important consequence of the uprising was the reduction of the Indian element of the army from 238,000 in 1857 to 140,000 by 1863. Recruitment also tended to take place among the 'martial races' of Nepal and the Punjab, who had proved their loyalty during the uprising. All artillery, moreover, was kept firmly in European hands. More constructive and imaginative measures were required, however, to guard against a repetition of the events of 1857.

In 1860, the government of India described the rulers of the princely Indian states as 'breakwaters to the storm which would otherwise have swept over us in one great wave'.[19] Nevertheless, it was widely recognised that in permitting Dalhousie's policy of lapse (see above, p. 53), Britain had courted disaster. Dispossessed members of the princely order, the most famous of which was the rani of Jhansi, had thrown in their lot with the mutineers. In the aftermath of the uprising, princes were given the right to adopt heirs, thus preventing the possibility of their states lapsing to Britain. In November 1858, Queen Victoria promised to 'respect the rights, dignity, and honour of the native princes as our own'. Loyal princes were rewarded with grants of land and money, and a new honour, the Star of India, was created to bind the princely order to the empire. Moreover, the state of Mysore, which had been governed by Britain since 1831, was returned to princely rule. Another powerful group which Britain sought to cultivate were the traditional landowners. This was particularly evident in Oudh, the seat of the rebellion.

Although Canning issued a proclamation in March 1858 confiscating land in Oudh, the policy was soon modified. It was quickly realised that the pacification of the state could only be achieved by reaching an accommodation with the *taluqdars*. As a result, Canning's initial policy was reversed, so that the majority of *taluqdars* were reinstated in their former holdings. *Taluqdars* were also given local administrative powers. The general aim, as the secretary of state for India, Sir Charles Wood, emphasised, was to 'enlist on our side, and to employ in our service, those natives who have, from their birth or their position, a natural influence in the country'.[20] With similar intentions in mind, the Indian Councils Act of 1861 permitted Indians to sit on the viceroy's legislative council and made provision for provincial legislatures. Real power, however, remained with the British: until 1892 membership was by appointment rather than election, while the councils themselves were restricted to a purely consultative role.

In 1882, the viceroy, Lord Ripon, introduced his Resolution on Local Self-government, which introduced representative institutions to municipal and local boards. In no real sense was this measure designed to promote political advance in India. Rather it sought to increase the number of Indians who collaborated with the British, particularly in such unpopular tasks as raising local revenue. Indeed, Britain had no intention of weakening her hold on India. This sentiment was reinforced by India's growing economic importance to Britain from the second half of the nineteenth century. By 1913, 60 per cent of India's imports came from Britain, while India represented the single largest market for British goods. India was also of growing importance as an area for British investment. In 1870, a fifth of Britain's total overseas investment – around £160 million – was in India. By 1913, this figure had increased to £380 million. Much of this money went into railway construction and by 1880 over 8,500 miles of track had been built. The advent of the railway allowed quite ordinary people to travel outside their own immediate area. By so doing they began to realise that they belonged to a wider community, region, or even nation. The growing educational opportunities open to Indians also widened their horizons. In 1880, the Bengali lawyer Lal Mohan Ghose warned that 'as our intellectual faculties are developed, so are our aspirations, both personal and national, sharpened and stimulated'.[21] Educated Indians began to criticise the lack of opportunity afforded to them by the Indian civil service, as well as the scale of government expenditure on the army. It was not until 1885, however, that these concerns were given expression through an organisation with national aspirations.

The Indian National Congress came into existence on 28 December 1885 when 72 delegates gathered at Bombay with the aim of allowing 'the most earnest labourers in the cause of national progress to become personally known to each other'.[22] The early Congress members were drawn mainly from the ranks of the educated professional classes of the maritime provinces (Bengal, Madras and Bombay). Congress demands were moderate in nature, the movement as a whole entering a 'discreet dialogue' with the British.[23]

Despite the Congress' all-India pretensions, it was a movement which attracted support mainly from Hindus. Muslims, who formed 20 per cent of the population of British India, looked to their own organisations to represent them. Founded in 1875 by the educationalist Sir Syed Ahmed Khan, the Muhammadan

Anglo-Oriental College at Aligarh directed much early Muslim political activity. Many of those who went on to form the All-India Muslim League in 1906 had been nurtured by Sir Syed's college. Muslims' tendency to organise along religious lines can be explained in a number of ways.[24] First, they were seeking to maintain their privileged position in areas such as the United Provinces in Northern India, where they formed a mere 14 per cent of the population. Furthermore, Muslims' sense of separateness was enhanced by a sharpening of Hindu religious identity towards the end of the nineteenth century. In seeking to come to terms with Western imperial domination, moreover, Indian Muslims experienced their own religious revival. British recognition of Muslim separatism came in the Morley–Minto Reforms of 1909, named after the secretary of state for India and the viceroy. While enlarging the elective element on provincial legislatures, these reforms also established separate electorates for Muslims. To what extent can British concessions to Muslims be seen as another attempt to attract Indian collaborators to the empire?

Document case study

5.1 Letter from Jeremy Bentham to Ram Mohan Roy (Bengali religious and social reformer), undated

For these many years the grand object of his [James Mill's] ambition has been to provide for British India, in the room of the abominable existing system, a good system of judicial procedure, with a judicial establishment adequate to the administration of it; and for the composition of it his reliance has all along been, and continues to be, on me.

Source: Eric Stokes, *The English Utilitarians and India*, Oxford, 1959, p. 147

5.2 Minute by Sir Thomas Munro, 31 December 1824

The ruling vice of our government is innovation; and its innovation has been so little guided by a knowledge of the people, that though made after what was thought by us to be mature discussion, it must appear to them as little better than the result of mere caprice. We have, in our anxiety to make every thing as English as possible in a country which resembles England in nothing, attempted to create at once, throughout extensive provinces, a kind of landed property which had never existed in them.

Source: Frederick Madden and David Fieldhouse (eds.), *Imperial reconstruction, 1740–1840: the evolution of alternative systems of government*, New York, 1987, p. 241

5.3 James Mill: evidence to the Commons' select committee, 16 February 1832

The princes exercise all the power that is left them to exercise as mere trustees of ours and unfortunately, they are very bad trustees . . . In my opinion the best thing for the happiness of the people is that our government should be nominally, as well as really, extended over those territories; that our own modes of governing should be adopted and our own people put in charge of the government.

Source: Frederick Madden and David Fieldhouse (eds.), *Imperial reconstruction, 1740–1840: the evolution of alternative systems of government*, New York, 1987, p. 246

5.4 Viceroy Canning to Sir Charles Wood (secretary of state for India), 13 June 1860

If we are wise we shall lose no time in binding to ourselves the Chiefs, landholders, great and small, and the wealthy classes (these last will follow in the wake of the first) by stronger and more substantial ties. We must impress them all with this plain conviction, that come what may, the fall of our power will be no gain to them.

Source: Frederick Madden and David Fieldhouse (eds.), *The dependent empire and Ireland, 1840–1900: advance and retreat in representative self-government*, New York, 1991, p. 80

5.5 Speech by Lord Cranborne (secretary of state for India, June 1866–March 1867), 24 May 1867

The general concurrence of those who know India best is that a number of well-governed small Native States are in the highest degree advantageous to the development of the political and moral condition of the people of India . . . I am not by this denying that our mission in India is to reduce to order, to civilise and develop the Native governments we find there. But I demur to that wholesale condemnation of a system of government which would be utterly intolerable on our own soil, but which has grown up amongst the people subjected to it. It has a fitness and congeniality for them impossible for us adequately to realise, but which compensates them to an enormous degree for the material evils which its rudeness in a great many cases produces.

Source: Frederick Madden and David Fieldhouse (eds.), *The dependent empire and Ireland, 1840–1900: advance and retreat in representative self-government*, New York, 1991, pp. 87, 88

5.6 Letter from Evelyn Baring (finance member, government of India), 25 September 1882

I do not see how we could move more cautiously and tentatively than we are moving . . . The idea that we are going too fast is a phantom . . . We shall not subvert the British Empire by allowing the Bengali Baboo [Indian clark] to discuss his own schools and drains. Rather shall we afford him a safety-valve if we turn his attention to such innocuous subjects.

Source: Anil Seal, *The emergence of Indian nationalism: competition and collaboration in the later nineteenth century*, Cambridge, 1968, p. 156

5.7 Letter from Sir Syed Ahmed Khan to Badruddin Tyabji, 24 January 1888

Badruddin Tyabji was a Bengali Muslim who sought to reconcile his co-religionists to the Indian National Congress.

I do not understand what the words 'national Congress' mean. Is it supposed that the different castes and creeds living in India belong to one nation, or can become one nation, and their aims and aspirations be one and the same? I think it is quite impossible and when it is impossible there can be no such thing as a national congress, nor can it be of equal benefit to all peoples.

You regard the doings of the misnamed National Congress as beneficial to India, but I am sorry to say that I regard them as not only injurious to our own community but also to India at large.

Source: B. N. Pandey (ed.), *The Indian nationalist movement, 1885–1947*, London, 1979, p. 15

Document case-study questions

1 Compare the attitudes towards reform in India in 5.1 with those in 5.2.

2 In what ways do the views of James Mill about indigenous institutions in 5.3 differ from those of Viceroy Canning in 5.4 and Lord Cranborne in 5.5?

3 What conclusions can be drawn from 5.6 about British attitudes towards Indian participation in government?

4 Comment on the significance of Sir Syed Ahmed Khan's views on the Congress in 5.7.

Notes and references

1 Thomas R. Metcalf, *The aftermath of revolt: India, 1857–1870*, New Delhi, 1990 (first published 1964), p. 9.

2 Cited in Ramsay Muir (ed.), *The making of British India, 1756–1858*, Manchester, 1915, p. 284.

3 Eric Stokes, *The English Utilitarians and India*, Oxford, 1959, p. 51.

4 George D. Bearce, *British attitudes towards India, 1784–1858*, Westport, 1982 (first published 1961), p. 162.

5 Bearce, *British attitudes*, p. 179.

6 Thomas R. Metcalf, *Ideologies of the raj*, Cambridge, 1994, p. 34.

7 Metcalf, *Aftermath of revolt*, p. 22.

8 Muir, *The making of British India*, p. 353.

9 Muir, *The making of British India*, p. 378.

10 Judith M. Brown, *Modern India: the origins of an Asian democracy*, Oxford, 1985, p. 82.

11 Eric Stokes, *The peasant armed: the Indian revolt of 1857*, Oxford, 1986, p. 4.

12 Metcalf, *Aftermath of revolt*, p. 73.

13 Neil Charlesworth, *British rule and the Indian economy, 1800–1914*, London, 1982, p. 32.

14 Metcalf, *Aftermath of revolt*, p. 61.

15 Eric Stokes, *The peasant and the raj: studies in agrarian society and peasant rebellion in colonial India*, Cambridge, 1978, p. 161. See also Stokes, *The peasant armed*, p. 205.

16 Stokes, *The peasant and the raj*, p. 187.

17 Stokes, *The peasant and the raj*, p. 185.

18 Metcalf, *Ideologies*, p. 45.

19 Brown, *Modern India*, p. 133.

20 Metcalf, *Aftermath of revolt*, p. 172.

21 Brown, *Modern India*, p. 150.

22 Gordon Johnson, *Provincial politics and Indian nationalism: Bombay and the Indian National Congress, 1880 to 1915*, Cambridge, 1973, p. 5.

23 Francis Robinson, 'The Indian National Congress', *History Today*, vol. 32 (1982): 33.

24 See Francis Robinson, *Separatism among Indian Muslims: the politics of the United Provinces' Muslims, 1860–1923*, Cambridge, 1974.

6 Imperialism and nationalism in India

Key dates

1915   Gandhi's return to India

1916   Lucknow Pact

1919   Montagu–Chelmsford Reforms
       Rowlatt Acts

1935   India Act

1940   Lahore Resolution

1942   Cripps Mission
       Quit India movement

1947   Transfer of power and partition of India

Early nationalist forces had first appeared on the Indian political scene in the late nineteenth century. Elitist in character and moderate in their demands, they presented little real threat to the British raj. However, the experience of the global war between 1914 and 1918 transformed the nature of the nationalist forces ranged against Britain. More broadly based and strident, they began to challenge the British for power in India. Britain responded by making a series of constitutional concessions in provincial government while retaining control at the centre. It was to take another world war, and a consequent reassessment of her interests in India, before Britain was prepared to bring her imperial presence to an end.

The Congress and the raj

On the outbreak of the First World War, India presented an image of impressive loyalty. Politicians and princes were conspicuous in their declarations of fealty to Britain and in the practical help which they provided. In 1917, the government of India made a gift of £100 million towards the cost of the war. Moreover, nearly 1,200,000 Indian volunteers were recruited for service in the army. However, the long-term effects of the war had the effect of loosening imperial ties.

Casting his thoughts back to the Seven Years War, Lord Milner of the British War Cabinet noted in 1915 that 'on a previous and most disastrous occasion it was not war – not the strain of war – which disrupted the Empire, but the aftermath of war'.[1] Milner's warning proved prophetic. After 1918, Indian acquiescence in British rule was increasingly replaced by resistance. Reflecting the changing attitudes, Madan Mohan Malaviya, a leading Congress politician, remarked in 1917: 'I venture to say that the war has put the clock . . . fifty years forward.'[2] In the same year, M. K. Gandhi launched his first campaign of passive resistance, or *satyagraha*.

Born in 1869, Gandhi received a legal training in Britain before returning to India to take up a career in law. Nothing in his early professional life suggested that he was destined to play a central role in Indian public affairs. Too nervous to speak in his first case, his career foundered until the opportunity arose in 1893 to become legal adviser to an Indian firm operating in South Africa. He soon experienced prejudice, being ejected from a train on account of his colour as he travelled from Durban to Pretoria. Appalled at such intolerance, he began campaigning on behalf of South Africa's oppressed Indian community. While in Africa, Gandhi developed *satyagraha*, or non-violent resistance, a tactic which he employed on his return to India in 1915. His first *satyagraha* campaign was conducted in northern Bihar on behalf of tenant-cultivators who were being exploited by British indigo-planters. In March 1919, Gandhi, who was rapidly establishing himself as the central figure in Congress politics, called for a national *satyagraha* following the introduction of the Rowlatt Acts, which extended wartime restrictions on civil liberties into the period of peace. Tensions were heightened in April when Brigadier-General Reginald Dyer ordered his men to fire on demonstrators in the Punjabi town of Amritsar, leaving 400 dead and over 1,000 wounded. The challenge to British authority was made all the more acute by an alliance between Hindus and Muslims which Gandhi engineered in 1920.

Despite being a Hindu, Gandhi sought to foster links with Muslims. As early as 1905, Gandhi had emphasised the 'necessity for perfect unity and brotherliness between all sections of the Indian community'.[3] Simultaneous meetings of the Indian National Congress and the Muslim League in Bombay in December 1915 had paved the way for a greater degree of mutual understanding. A year later, the new spirit of co-operation between the two organisations was cemented by the Lucknow Pact. The Congress accepted separate electorates and a bargain was struck over the distribution of seats in provincial councils. Gandhi sought to build on this demonstration of Hindu–Muslim solidarity. In 1919, he lent his support to the Khilafat movement, a body of Indian Muslims who were incensed at Britain's treatment of the spiritual head of Islam, the Sultan of Turkey, at the end of the First World War. In June 1920, the Central Khilafat Committee called for a programme of non-cooperation, which the Congress, after much soul-searching, joined. Although Gandhi called off the campaign at the beginning of 1922 amid mounting violence, the experience of the previous two years had transformed the Congress into a mass movement.

In 1892, the future viceroy of India, Lord Curzon, had remarked that 'the constituency which the Congress Party represents cannot be described as otherwise than a microscopic minority of the total population'.[4] Thirty years later, the same claim could not be made with any accuracy. By 1922, Congress had a membership of nearly two million drawn not merely from the elite but also from the lower reaches of society. Reflecting the change in the composition of the party, a British police official observed: 'The intelligentsia, which dominated earlier Congresses, seems to have been swamped in a mass of semi-educated persons swept up from all parts of India.'[5] The ability of the Congress to attract the popular element to its banner can be explained largely with reference to the repercussions of the First World War. Many Indian soldiers returned home dissatisfied with their treatment during the war. The general price rises and tax increases as a result of war affected the lives of every man and woman in India. Furthermore, Congress leaders were able to use the liberal wartime rhetoric of Britain and her allies to appeal to the masses and demand greater freedoms for India. Britain's response to such demands was to make concessions to Indian nationalist opinion.

In August 1917, the secretary of state for India, Edwin Montagu, declared the aim of British policy to be 'the progressive realisation of responsible government in India as an integral part of the British Empire'. Two years later, the Montagu–Chelmsford Reforms, named after the secretary of state and his viceroy, attempted to give substance to this undertaking. Directly elected majorities were introduced in the provincial and central legislative councils. While the viceroy and his executive remained supreme at the centre, a system of dyarchy was established in the provinces whereby certain local matters, such as agriculture, education and public works, were transferred to Indian ministers responsible to provincial legislatures. In 1927, a commission under the chairmanship of Sir John Simon was instituted to examine the workings of the Montagu–Chelmsford Reforms. Two years later, the viceroy, Lord Irwin, declared that 'the natural issue of India's constitutional progress . . . is the attainment of Dominion status'. After six further years of often tortuous discussions, the 1935 India Act was passed under which dyarchy in the provinces was replaced by full responsible government. The Act also envisaged the establishment of a federation between princely and British India, with an elected federal assembly enjoying dyarchical powers in central government. British motives in devolving power, however, have been questioned by historians.

John Gallagher argues that the Montagu–Chelmsford Reforms were planned as 'a way of diverting Indian political attention from the national, the all-India stage, and directing it to provincial affairs'.[6] In a similar vein, Carl Bridge has described the reforms as restructuring the raj 'in order better to safeguard the essentials of the British position'.[7] John Darwin, moreover, has argued that 'The 1935 Act clearly signalled London's determination that India should be held within the imperial system and that the benefits of a close coordination of India's foreign and defence policies with those of the mother-country should be preserved'.[8] B. R. Tomlinson, furthermore, has characterised the progress of constitutional advance as being 'determined by the need to attract Indian collaborators to the Raj, swell the revenues and maintain the political security of British rule, leaving the government of India free to fulfill its imperial role'.[9]

Indeed, under the terms of the 1935 Act, India's defence and foreign relations were reserved to the viceroy's prerogative. Further safeguards were provided by the stipulation that the proposed federation would only come into operation once half the princes had formally acceded to it. Cautious by nature and fearful of Congress influence in their states, the princes shied away from entering the federation.[10] Even if a sufficient number of princes had acceded, they would have represented a grouping loyal to the imperial connection – Gandhi once dismissed them as 'British officers in Indian dress'.[11] Despite Britain's elaborate efforts to hold India to the empire, the inter-war years witnessed an erosion in the subcontinent's imperial value.

The ending of hostilities in 1918 brought no respite for the government of India. With over a quarter of a million men in the Middle East region alone, a reduction in military expenditure proved impossible. In 1920, Britain asked the government of India to provide additional forces to compensate for the withdrawal of British troops from Iraq, the cost of which would have pushed India's spending on the army to £60 million a year, or 40 per cent of net Indian revenues. In response, Montagu fulminated: 'we must definitely get out of our heads the vague idea, too often entertained, that India is an inexhaustible reservoir from which men and money can be drawn towards the support of Imperial resources or in pursuance of Imperial strategy'.[12] With such considerations in mind, the Iraq garrison scheme was abandoned. In January 1923, the British cabinet conceded that 'the Indian Army cannot be treated as if it were absolutely at the disposal of His Majesty's Government for service outside India'.[13] As war loomed in the late 1930s, the Chatfield Committee was appointed to examine India's role in imperial defence, reaching the conclusion that Britain should contribute £34 million towards the costs of modernising the Indian Army. In November 1939, the Defence Expenditure Agreement established that the government of India would only pay for the direct costs of defending India. The costs of using the Indian Army for imperial purposes would have to be borne by Britain. As a result of this agreement, Britain's indebtedness to India exceeded £1,300 million by the end of the Second World War. If India's military value to Britain was declining in the inter-war years, so too was her economic worth.

As India's national debt soared during First World War, the government of India began searching for new sources of revenue. Following India's £100 million contribution to the British war effort in 1917, London permitted Delhi to increase to 7.5 per cent the tariff on cotton goods, Britain's principal export to India. Under the fiscal autonomy agreement of 1919, Britain conceded to the government of India the right to set India's tariffs. When additional revenue was required the government of India tended to turn to tariff increases, which fell on British manufacturers, rather than to the more politically sensitive expedient of raising local income tax. With such considerations in mind, the cotton tariff was raised to 11 per cent in 1921, 15 per cent in 1930, and 20 per cent in 1931.

A combination of tariff increases, Congress-led boycotts of British goods and uncompetitive prices saw sales of British cloth in India slump from 1,248 million yards in 1929 to only 376 million yards in 1931. In that year, and again between

1933 and 1938, India enjoyed a balance of payments surplus in commodities with Britain. As B. R. Tomlinson has noted: 'Whatever stake Britain might once have had in India as a colonial market, the boot was on the other foot by 1939.'[14] Moreover, Britain's ability to manipulate the Indian economy for imperial purposes was further weakened by the cabinet's decision at the end of 1932 to transfer control of Indian finance from the secretary of state to the viceroy. In the short term, such concessions helped to keep India within the empire. As we have seen, however, their long-term consequences eroded India's imperial value. Furthermore, Britain's nationalist opponents were able to exploit the new constitutional structures in order to 'raise the financial and moral price which the British would have to pay if they wished to remain'.[15] This was achieved in a number of ways.

Although the central legislative assembly established by the Montagu–Chelmsford Reforms enjoyed few real powers, it became a forum for airing Indian grievances and expressing dissatisfaction with British rule. 'My task had been', complained the viceroy, Lord Reading, in the early 1920s, 'to govern with a parliament in which there is always a large majority against the Government.'[16] These problems were compounded by the devolution of power following the 1935 India Act. In 1937, the first elections to be held under the Act left Congress in power in 7 provinces out of 11. The new Congress ministries undermined the economic basis of the raj by jealously guarding revenues from locally raised taxes and remitting to central government, which the British still dominated, as little as possible. Moreover, Britain's plans to divert Indian attention into provincial politics were restricted by the decision of all-India Congress figures not to stand for election in 1937. On the outbreak of the Second World War, however, India's residual worth, its strategic and military potential, were once more realised.

During the war years, India represented a vital base for operations in the Middle East and Southeast Asia. Moreover, the Indian Army's strength increased from 205,058 in October 1939 to over two and a quarter million by July 1945. The pursuit of victory, however, had the effect of hastening Britain's departure from the subcontinent.

Independence and partition

On 3 September 1939, the viceroy, Lord Linlithgow, declared war against Germany without consulting any Indian leaders. In protest, the Congress ministries resigned from office. Linlithgow's 'August Offer' of 1940, which included dominion status at an unspecified future time and the inclusion of more Indians on the viceroy's executive council, failed to impress Congress. A more serious attempt at conciliation occurred during the Cripps Mission of March–April 1942.

With the war going badly for Britain, Sir Stafford Cripps, a Labour member of the British coalition government, was dispatched to India in an effort to secure Congress co-operation. Cripps offered greater Indian participation in the conduct of the war, including an Indianised executive that would function as a cabinet, as well as the promise of Indian independence once peace had been restored. Although likened by Gandhi to drawing a 'post-dated cheque on a crashing bank',[17] Cripps' proposals were given serious consideration by the chief Congress negotiators, Congress president A. K. Azad, and future Indian prime minister Jawaharlal Nehru. With agreement within tantalising reach, negotiations foundered. Fearing that Cripps had gone too far, the British premier, Winston Churchill, withdrew Cripps' freedom to negotiate on the executive, precipitating the collapse of the talks. In the wake of this failure, Congress launched its 'Quit India' campaign.

In August 1942, Congress endorsed Gandhi's resolution calling on Britain to 'Quit India' and allow Indians to negotiate with the Japanese. The arrest of leading Congress members and the subsequent banning of the organisation sparked widespread anti-British violence in northern India of the type not witnessed since 1857. With the assistance of British troops, the authorities managed to re-establish order by the beginning of 1943. Congress' sudden removal from the political scene provided the Muslim League with a unique opportunity to enhance its standing.

The alliance between Congress and League, symbolised by the Lucknow Pact and Khilafat movement, did not last long. By 1923, only 3.6 per cent of Congress delegates were Muslims, and a year later the two organisations met separately for the first time since 1920. League fortunes dwindled in the inter-war years. Its claim to represent Muslims was discredited at the 1937 elections: it captured only 2 out of 84 reserved constituencies in the Punjab and 3 from 33 in Sind, and it failed to win a single seat in the North-West Frontier Province.[18] In the face of such reverses, the League leader, Mohammad Ali Jinnah, sought to rally Muslim support. In March 1940, he issued the Lahore Resolution, which demanded that 'areas in which Muslims are numerically in a majority, as in the north-western and eastern zones of India, should be grouped to constitute "independent States" in which the constituent units shall be autonomous and sovereign'.

Although the Resolution has traditionally been seen as a demand for a separate Muslim homeland (Pakistan), Ayesha Jalal argues that Jinnah merely saw it as a 'bargaining counter' designed to force the Congress to share power at the centre.[19] The realisation of Pakistan, however, received a boost in 1942 when Cripps recognised the right of provinces to secede from an independent India. League claims to represent Muslims were enhanced when it was invited to form governments in Bengal, Sind, Assam and North-West Frontier Province in the wake of Congress' Quit India movement. The League's new status was reflected in the winter elections of 1945–46, which saw it winning all the Muslim seats in the central legislative assembly and 439 out of 494 seats reserved for Muslims in provincial legislatures. Meanwhile, the British imperial position in India was visibly crumbling.

The trial of former members of the Indian National Army (INA), an anti-British force which had fought alongside the Japanese during the Second World War, became a focus of discontent. In mid-February 1946, Calcutta descended into anarchy after sentence was passed on a former INA soldier. Within days, the Royal Indian Navy mutinied in Bombay, precipitating a general strike in the city. There followed widespread disturbances, which required two battalions of troops to quell. Amid growing lawlessness, the Labour government of Clement Attlee, which had come to power in 1945, dispatched a cabinet mission to India in March 1946. The failure of the cabinet mission to reach agreement with the two major parties on the transfer of power to a single successor state merely presaged further violence. By 19 August, at least 4,000 had been killed and 10,000 injured in Calcutta alone. Britain's dwindling military resources, coupled with growing doubts about the loyalty of the Indian Army, made the security situation yet more dangerous.[20]

Determined to extricate Britain from her Indian bondage, Attlee pledged on 20 February 1947 that Britain would withdraw from India no later than June of the following year. He also announced the appointment of Lord Mountbatten as Britain's last viceroy. Within a short time of his arrival in India, Mountbatten realised that even the truncated timetable envisaged by Attlee would leave Britain in a precarious position. 'The only conclusion that I have been able to come to is that unless I act quickly I may well find the real beginnings of a civil war on my hands', he wrote at the beginning of April.[21] On 3 June, Mountbatten announced that independence would be granted at midnight on 14–15 August. Despite previously dismissing the concept of Pakistan as 'sheer madness', [22] Mount-batten also accepted the partition of India. This still left the apparently intractable problem of the princely Indian states. On 25 July, Mountbatten persuaded a majority of princes to accede to either India or Pakistan.[23] The transfer of power was accompanied, however, by renewed communal violence, which prompted Gandhi's comment: 'We have well-nigh turned into beasts.'[24] To what extent was British policy over the previous forty years responsible for the unbridgeable divide between Muslims and Hindus?

Document case study

6.1 Memorandum on Indian self-government by Lord Curzon (viceroy, 1899–1905), 2 July 1917

What do we mean by self-government for India? We do not mean that India, either now or in any future that can be reasonably predicted, will become a single autonomous or *quasi*-autonomous political unit, in which Indians will be universally substituted for British administrators, and the 250 millions of Indian peoples of every race, religion, and state of development – outside the Native States – will constitute a self-governing dominion under the suzerainty, either more or less effective, of the British Crown. Such an aspiration, in the present phase of Indian evolution, is the wildest of dreams; and the belief that it can be attained, almost at a bound, is doomed to irretrievable disappointment.

Source: Frederick Madden and John Darwin (eds.), *The dominions and India since 1900*, Westport, 1993, p. 677

6.2 Letter from Lord Linlithgow to Lord Zetland (secretary of state for India, 1935– 40), 21 December 1939

After all we framed the constitution as it stands in the Act of 1935 because we thought that way the best way – given the political position in both countries – of maintaining British influence in India. It is no part of our policy, I take it, to expedite in India constitutional changes for their own sake, or gratuitously to hurry the handing over of the controls to Indian hands at any rate faster than that which we regard as best calculated, on the long view, to hold India to the Empire.

Source: Carl Bridge, *Holding India to the empire: the British Conservative Party and the 1935 constitution*, New Delhi, 1986, p. 153

6.3 Speech delivered by Mohammad Ali Jinnah in Calcutta on 3 January 1937

Mr Jawaharlal Nehru is reported to have said that there are only two parties in India – the Government and the Congress – and others must line up. I refuse to line up with the Congress, I refuse to accept this proposition. There is a third party in this country and that is Muslim India . . . We are willing as equal partners to come to a settlement with our sister communities in the interest of India.

Source: P. N. Chopra (ed.), *Towards freedom, 1937–47: volume 1: experiment with provincial autonomy*, New Delhi, 1985, p. 14

6.4 Nehru's rebuttal of Jinnah's concept of third party, 10 January 1937

The Congress represents Indian nationalism and is thus charged with historic destiny. Because of this, it is the only organisation which has developed a vast prestige in India and the strength and will to stand up against British imperialism. Thus in the final analysis, there are only two forces in India today – British imperialism and the Congress representing Indian nationalism . . . The communal groupings have no such real importance in spite of occasional importance being thrust upon them.

Source: P. N. Chopra (ed.), *Towards freedom, 1937–47: volume 1: experiment with provincial autonomy*, New Delhi, 1985, pp. 24–25

6.5 'India: constitutional position': cabinet conclusions, 10 December 1946

The strength of British forces in India was not great. And the Indian Army, though the Commander-in-Chief had great personal influence with it, could not fairly be expected to prove a reliable instrument for maintaining public order in conditions tantamount to civil war. One thing was quite certain viz., that we could not put back the clock and introduce a period of firm British rule. Neither the military nor the administrative machine in India was any longer capable of this.

Source: CAB 128/8, cited in Ronald Hyam (ed.), *The Labour government and the end of empire, 1945–51*, part 1, London, 1992, pp. 31–32

6.6 Entry in the journal of Lord Wavell (viceroy, 1943–47), 31 December 1946

[T]he administration has declined, and the machine in the Centre is hardly working at all now, my ministers are too busy with politics. And while the British are still legally and morally responsible for what happens in India, we have lost nearly all power to control events; we are simply running on the momentum of our previous prestige. The loyalty of the Police is doubtful in some of the Provinces, they are tinged with communalism; fortunately the Indian Army seems unaffected so far, but it can hardly remain so indefinitely, if communal tension continues.

Source: Penderel Moon (ed.), *Wavell: the viceroy's journal*, London, 1973, p. 402

6.7 Note on India by Lord Ismay (Mountbatten's chief of staff), 18 March–18 July 1947

Before I left England on 18th March, I was doubtful whether a mistake had not been made in fixing the date for the transfer of power to Indian hands as early as June, 1948. I had been in India for a week before it was borne in on me that so far from being too early, it was too late. I got the impression that in a very short time we should find ourselves still saddled with tremendous responsibilities, but equipped with no power wherewith to discharge them. The few British officials that were still in service were at the end of their tether . . . British arms were represented by little more than token forces.

Source: R. J. Moore, *Escape from empire: the Attlee government and the Indian problem*, Oxford, 1983, p. 238

6.8 Dalton's explanation for the British withdrawal from India

Dalton was chancellor of the exchequer in Attlee's post-war Labour government.

24 February 1947

If you are in a place where you are not wanted, and where you have not got the force, or perhaps the will, to squash those who don't want you, the only thing to do is to come out . . . The Tories are making a good deal of a hoot about India, but I don't believe that one person in a hundred thousand in this country cares tuppence about it, as long as British people are not being mauled about out there.

Source: Hugh Dalton, *High tide and after: memoirs, 1945–1960*, London, 1962, p. 211

Document case-study questions

1 Compare Lord Curzon's views on the speed of constitutional advance in India in 6.1 with those of Lord Linlithgow in 6.2.

2 Which of the conflicting views on the Congress expressed in 6.3 and 6.4 do you find more convincing?

3 Evaluate the problems faced by Britain as described in 6.5, 6.6 and 6.7.

4 How adequate do you find Hugh Dalton's explanation in 6.8 for Britain's withdrawal from India?

Notes and references

1 A. J. Stockwell, 'The war and the British empire', in John Turner (ed.), *Britain and the First World War*, London, 1988, p. 44.

2 Judith M. Brown, *Modern India: the origins of an Asian democracy*, Oxford, 1985, p. 191.

3 Judith M. Brown, *Gandhi: prisoner of hope*, New Haven, 1989, p. 48.

4 Brown, *Modern India*, p. 139.

5 Cited in Robin Jeffrey, 'India: independence and the rich peasant', in Robin Jeffrey (ed.), *Asia – the winning of independence*, Basingstoke, 1981, p. 83.

6 John Gallagher, *The decline, revival and fall of the British Empire*, Cambridge, 1982, p. 101. See also John Gallagher and Anil Seal, 'Britain and India between the wars', *Modern Asian Studies*, vol. 15 (1981): 395.

7 Carl Bridge, *Holding India to the empire: the British Conservative Party and the 1935 constitution*, New Delhi, 1986, p. 5.

8 John Darwin, 'Imperialism in decline? Tendencies in British imperial policy between the wars', *Historical Journal*, vol. 23 (1980): 676.

9 B. R. Tomlinson, 'India and the British empire, 1880–1935', *Indian Economic and Social History Review*, vol. 12 (1975): 376.

10 See S. R. Ashton, 'Federal negotiations with the Indian princes, 1935–1939', *Journal of Imperial and Commonwealth History*, vol. 9 (1981): 169–92.

11 Nicholas Mansergh, *The Commonwealth experience: volume 2: from British to multiracial Commonwealth*, London, 1982, p. 114.

12 B. R. Tomlinson, *The political economy of the raj, 1914–1947: the economics of decolonization in India*, London, 1979, p. 115.

13 B. R. Tomlinson, *The Indian National Congress and the raj, 1929–1942*, London, 1976, p. 13.

14 Tomlinson, 'India and the British empire, 1880–1935', p. 369.

15 Francis Robinson, 'The Indian National Congress', *History Today*, vol. 32 (1982): 34.

16 Tomlinson, *Indian National Congress*, p. 14.

17 Martin Kitchen, *The British Empire and Commonwealth: a short history*, Basingstoke, 1996, p. 89.

18 Sumit Sarkar, *Modern India, 1885–1947*, Basingstoke, 1989, p. 349.

19 Ayesha Jalal, *The sole spokesman: Jinnah, the Muslim League and the demand for Pakistan*, Cambridge, 1985, pp. 57–60.

20 See Hugh Tinker, 'The contraction of empire in Asia, 1945–48: the military dimension', *Journal of Imperial and Commonwealth History*, vol. 16 (1988): 218–33.

21 Nicholas Mansergh (ed.), *Constitutional relations between Britain and India: the transfer of power, 1942–7*, 12 vols., London, 1981, vol. 10, p. 91.

22 R. J. Moore, *Endgames of empire: studies in Britain's Indian problem*, Delhi, 1988, p. 140.

23 See Ian Copland, 'Lord Mountbatten and the integration of the Indian states: a reappraisal', *Journal of Imperial and Commonwealth History*, vol. 21 (1993): 385–408.

24 Brown, *Gandhi*, p. 375.

7 Britain's imperial century, 1815–1914

Key dates

1839–42 First Opium War
1846 Repeal of the Corn Laws
1849 Repeal of the Navigation Acts
1856–60 Second Opium War
1869 Opening of the Suez Canal
1876 Queen Victoria becomes Empress of India
1882 British occupation of Egypt
1884–85 Berlin Conference
1902 Publication of J. A. Hobson's *Imperialism: a study*

The period from 1815 to 1914 has been seen as Britain's 'imperial century'. The last quarter of the nineteenth century in particular saw dramatic extensions of British territory in Africa and Southeast Asia. Indeed, it can be suggested that these years marked a decisive phase in the establishment of Britain's identity as an imperial power. Whether the costs of maintaining her inflated empire outweighed the benefits is a question which has exercised historians. Historical attention has also focused on areas which, while outside formal British control, were nevertheless under imperial influence. Some have even identified the existence of a vast 'informal empire'.

The 'imperialism of free trade'

Until the 1950s, it was generally assumed that the mid-nineteenth century witnessed an era of indifference to empire. This attitude stemmed from the rise of free trade and the decline of old mercantilism. In 1846, the Corn Laws, which had provided tariff protection to British agriculture, were repealed. Three years later, the Navigation Acts, which had underpinned the protectionist system, were also repealed. The practical effects of the introduction of free trade were the abolition of import duties, colonial preferences and shipping restrictions.

Anticipating the results of free trade, T. B. Macaulay declared in 1842: 'we might supply the whole world with manufactures and have almost a monopoly of the trade of the world'.[1] Such confidence in the strength of the British economy led some contemporaries to doubt the value of empire, the eighteenth-century rationale for which had been the provision of guaranteed markets for British goods. The doubters became associated with the Manchester School of economists led by Richard Cobden. Cobden was a consistent critic of empire who in the aftermath of the Indian uprising of 1857 proclaimed that it would 'be a happy day when England has not an acre of territory in Continental Asia'.[2] While anti-imperial views did exist in the mid-Victorian age, their influence on British imperial policy is less certain.

In 1953, John Gallagher and Ronald Robinson published their controversial article, 'The imperialism of free trade'. As the title suggests, they sought to question the notion that free trade heralded an age of anti-imperialism. 'Far from being an era of "indifference"', they argue, 'the mid-Victorian years were the decisive stage in the history of British expansion overseas'.[3] They justify their interpretation in a number of ways. First, they point to the extension of formal British territory during the free-trading mid-Victorian years: Oudh, Lower Burma and Kowloon in Asia; Basutoland and Griqualand in southern Africa; and Lagos and the neighbourhood of Sierra Leone in West Africa. Second, they indicate the growth of a huge 'informal empire' which while not directly ruled by Britain was nevertheless under her imperial sway. Indeed, they argue that regarding only territory under Britain's direct control as part of the empire is 'rather like judging the size and character of icebergs solely from the parts above the water-line'.[4] In Gallagher and Robinson's analysis, the informal empire stemmed from the integration of new regions into Britain's expanding economy. 'Once entry had been forced into Latin America, China and the Balkans', they contend, 'the task was to encourage stable governments as good investment risks, just as in weaker or unsatisfactory states it was considered necessary to coerce them into more co-operative attitudes.'[5] Britain's recognition in the 1820s of the independence of the emerging Latin American republics was designed to 'shatter the Spanish trade monopoly, and to gain informal supremacy'.[6] Gallagher and Robinson conclude that the 'usual summing up of the policy of the free trade empire as "trade not rule" should read "trade with informal control if possible; trade with rule when necessary".[7] Not surprisingly, the Robinson and Gallagher thesis has been subjected to close scrutiny. D. C. M. Platt has been one of their principal critics.

In Platt's view, Gallagher and Robinson have exaggerated the extent to which the British government was prepared to intervene in support of her economic interests. 'Fair and equal treatment', stresses Platt, 'not *favoured* treatment, was what British diplomacy aimed to achieve for British trade.'[8] Platt has also cast doubt on the extent of Britain's economic penetration of the 'informal empire' in the mid-Victorian years. In his analysis, the economic potential of areas such as China and Latin America was restricted by local resistance to British manufactures and the lack of a return trade in locally produced commodities.[9] An evaluation of the relative merits of the arguments of Gallagher and Robinson, on the one hand, and Platt, on the other, is necessary to determine the viability of the term 'informal empire'.

As regards the preparedness of the British government to intervene in support of economic interests, it can be suggested that Platt overstates his case. While it is true that Britain rarely sought to secure exclusive economic privileges, Platt underestimates the extent of British interference in the internal affairs of those states identified by Gallagher and Robinson as being within the informal empire.

No matter how earnestly British statesmen might espouse non-intervention, a combination of poor communications, vague instructions and local instability provided British representatives with ample scope to act in defiance of official policy. In Brazil, Argentina and Central America in the 1840s, British diplomats, consuls, and naval officers became embroiled in local politics.[10] In China, moreover, Britons also became heavily involved in internal affairs. In 1854, for instance, a British-dominated customs agency was established, Sir Robert Hart acting as inspector-general of Chinese customs from 1863 to 1906. Britain also engaged in forceful interventions, the so-called Opium Wars of 1839–42 and 1856–60, in order to open China to greater trade. As a consequence of these wars, a number of treaty ports, through which unhindered trade could be conducted, were established. In the aftermath of the First Opium War, moreover, Hong Kong became a British colony. With a view to making China more responsive to Western demands, the British induced the Chinese imperial authorities to set up a modern foreign office, or *Tsungli-yamen*, in 1861. While Platt's characterisation of Britain as a non-interventionist power in the mid-Victorian years is open to question, it is equally uncertain whether the scale of British trade justifies Gallagher and Robinson's use of the term empire.

Gallagher and Robinson define imperialism as a 'political function' of the process of 'integrating new regions into the expanding economy'.[11] However, the process of Britain's economic integration with those areas of the world identified as being part of the informal empire was patchy and frequently attended by disappointment. In 1817, Lord Brougham told the House of Commons that, 'no field of enterprise was so magnificent in promise . . . as the vast continent of South America'.[12] These early expectations were soon frustrated. After an initial boom following independence, Latin America's relative importance to the British economy began to ebb, the region's share of Britain's export trade declining from 12.6 per cent in the mid-1820s to 8.8 per cent by the mid-1850s. A similar pattern can be discerned in relation to China which, despite the opening of the treaty ports in the mid-century, was becoming less important to British trade.[13] Explaining the contrast between expectations and reality, Sir Robert Hart noted: 'The Chinese have the best food in the world, rice; the best drink, tea; and best clothing, cotton, silk and fur. Possessing these staples, and their innumerable native adjuncts, they do not need to buy a penny's-worth elsewhere.'[14] Not only were the returns discouraging, but also British merchants, far from displacing their local rivals, were frequently forced to rely on them for access to domestic markets. Such a demonstrable lack of British economic dominance can be used to cast doubt on the existence of an informal empire in the mid-Victorian years. The concept of informal empire can be applied more successfully to the years leading up to the First World War.

'If Gallagher and Robinson overestimated the extent of Britain's informal empire in the mid-Victorian era', argue P. J. Cain and A. G. Hopkins, 'Platt has underestimated its size during the Edwardian period.'[15] Focusing on Latin America, Cain and Hopkins demonstrate that in contrast with the erosion of this region as a market for British manufactures from the late nineteenth century, its importance as a recipient of British capital was increasing. British holdings in Latin America grew from a modest £81 million in 1865 to reach the remarkable figure of £1,180, or 25 per cent of Britain's overseas investment, by 1913. Argentina alone received 41 per cent of British investment in Latin America. Likening this country to Canada and Australia, Cain and Hopkins have described it as an 'honorary dominion'. More generally, Cain and Hopkins contend that it was 'in the second half of the nineteenth century, and especially after 1870, that Britain's expanding financial power created a world-wide "invisible empire" which compensated for her dwindling economic influence in the United States and Europe'.[16] In attempting to establish a link between the export of capital and British overseas expansion, Cain and Hopkins have drawn on the work of early-twentieth-century writers.

Economics and empire

In his 1902 publication, *Imperialism: a study*, the economist J. A. Hobson propounded the 'surplus capital' theory of expansion. When domestic industry produced more capital than could be profitably reinvested in the domestic economy, he argued, financiers sought overseas outlets for their money. Such surplus capital derived from a maldistribution of wealth which left too much money in too few hands. Having invested in unsettled parts of the world, financiers pressed for British intervention to protect their investments. Summarising his thesis, Hobson declared: 'It is not too much to say that the modern foreign policy of Great Britain is primarily a struggle for profitable markets of investment' (see document 7.6). Hobson's ideas were later taken up by the Russian communist leader V. I. Lenin, in an attempt to demonstrate that imperialism was not only a natural corollary of capitalism, but also a sign of its ultimate and inevitable downfall. The incontestable fact that very little of Britain's total investments were placed in the new African and Asian territories acquired at the end of the nineteenth century appeared to discredit Hobson's and Lenin's arguments.[17] More recently, however, Hobson's and Lenin's assertion that imperialism derived from metropolitan economic forces has been revived, though in a modified form, by Cain and Hopkins.

'Explanations of imperialism ought to begin with a close study of economic structure and change in Britain', argue Cain and Hopkins.[18] In the past, however, they suggest that 'non-industrial forms of capitalist enterprise, particularly those in finance and commercial services, have not received the historical recognition they deserve'.[19] Despite the slow growth of manufacturing output after the mid-nineteenth century, the financial and service sectors of the economy experienced rapid expansion. In Cain and Hopkins' analysis, the link between Britain's expanding financial interests and empire was provided by 'gentlemanly capital-ists', landowners and financiers from the south of England who possessed the same social background and perceptions of national interest as the aristocratic governing class. Northern manufacturers, by contrast, were 'largely outside the circle of gentlemanly culture and did not "speak the same language" as the aristo-financial élite'.[20]

Applying their interpretation to the European partition of Africa at the end of the nineteenth century, Cain and Hopkins suggest that Britain's participation was dictated by a determination to protect her economic interests. In conse-quence, they focus on those areas of the continent, such as Egypt and southern Africa, where Britain's economic stake, especially her investments, was greatest. Referring to Britain's occupation of Egypt in 1882, for instance, Cain and Hopkins maintain that, 'British policy was assertive not because policy-makers were in the pockets of the bond-holders, but because they recognised the need to defend Britain's substantial economic interests'.[21] Cain and Hopkins' ideas, however, are open to a number of criticisms.[22]

In concentrating on finance, it can be suggested that Cain and Hopkins have focused on the 'gentlemanly capitalists' to the exclusion of other important influences on the course of British imperialism. Andrew Porter, for example, has demonstrated that strong regional centres such as West and Central Scotland and Lancashire developed extensive overseas connections. David Cannadine, furthermore, has stressed that Cain and Hopkins have drawn an artificial distinction between the industrial and financial-service sectors of the British economy, which were often complementary, not competing. Cannadine also emphasises that late-nineteenth-century British statesmen were not indifferent to the needs of industry, and that the financial service-sector did not speak with a single voice. In a similar vein, D. K. Fieldhouse has questioned the homo-geneity of the 'gentlemanly capitalist' class. In addition, he suggests that Cain and Hopkins have placed too much emphasis on the metropolitan centre at the expense of the imperial periphery. An emphasis on events on the imperial periphery is central to Gallagher and Robinson's explanation for the European partition of Africa. (See Map 4.)

'Scanning Europe for the causes', argue Gallagher and Robinson, 'the theorists of imperialism have been looking for the answers in the wrong places. The crucial changes that set all working took place in Africa itself.'[23] These changes centred on a series of local crises, the most important of which was the outbreak in 1881 of an army revolt led by Arabi Pasha against the ruler, or khedive, of Egypt. With the breakdown of indigenous authority, Britain was forced to intervene to protect her vital strategic interests in Egypt, more particularly the Suez Canal.

Completed in 1869, the Canal provided Britain with an alternative route to India and the East which was much quicker than either the Cape passage or overland routes through the Middle East. In 1875, the prime minister, Benjamin Disraeli, had acquired for Britain 177,000 out of 400,000 Suez Canal Company shares. By 1882, not only was more than 80% of Suez traffic British, but also

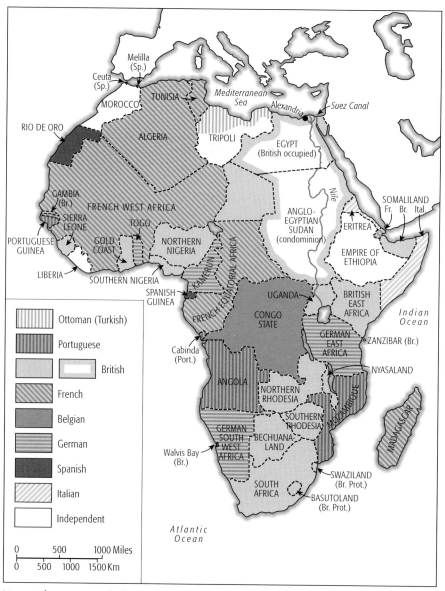

Map 4. The partition of Africa by 1902

13% of Britain's entire trade was passing through the Canal. In Gallagher and Robinson's analysis, the threat to the Canal posed by Arabi's revolt forced Britain to act. Summarising Britain's approach to the problem, they insist that: 'According to the dogmas of strategy, if Suez was in jeopardy, it must be protected at any cost.'[24] Britain's occupation of Egypt, however, had repercussions across Africa. 'From start to finish', contend Gallagher and Robinson, 'the partition of tropical Africa was driven by the persistent crisis in Egypt. When the

British entered Egypt on their own, the Scramble began; and as long as they stayed in Cairo, it continued until there was no more of Africa left to divide.'[25] In their opinion, the French, offended at Britain's unilateral action, embarked upon an expansionist policy in West Africa in order to provide both compensation and a means of forcing the British to leave Egypt. Prime minister Salisbury's decision in 1889 that Britain would remain in Egypt for the foreseeable future, argue Gallagher and Robinson, led to the second phase of the European partition of Africa in which Britain strove to keep the Nile valley and much of eastern Africa under her control in order strategically to protect Egypt. However, a number of criticisms can be levelled at this Egyptocentric thesis.

G. N. Sanderson has demonstrated that the partition of territory predated Britain's occupation of Egypt.[26] Prompted by concerns about the extension of British supremacy, the French in the 1870s began expanding their imperial presence, especially in West Africa, a development facilitated by the erosion of Britain's traditional naval dominance. Gallagher and Robinson's argument has also been weakened by A. G. Hopkins' contention that the French, far from being alienated by Britain's occupation of Egypt in 1882, congratulated the British for taking action that appeared to protect the lives and property of Frenchmen.[27] Moreover, it can be suggested that the Berlin Conference of 1884–85, rather than Britain's occupation of Egypt in 1882, began a new aggressive phase in the partition of Africa. Indeed, by establishing the doctrine of 'effective occupation', the Conference forced countries wishing to have a stake in Africa to establish a formal presence, rather than relying on claims to informal supremacy. The fact that other areas of the world, most notably Southeast Asia, were also partitioned at this time,[28] suggests that wider international forces were at work in the late nineteenth century than simply those connected with Britain's occupation of Egypt. Whether the British Empire in this period was a source of strength or weakness to Britain is a controversial question.

Despite the devotion to empire expressed by late-nineteenth-century politicians, historians have questioned the value of Britain's imperial presence. At the forefront of this reassessment have been Lance E. Davis and Robert A. Huttenback. As regards the financial benefits of empire, they seek to demonstrate that in the last twenty years of the nineteenth century British investment outside the empire yielded higher rates of return than investment in the empire. '[F]or the general investor in the years after 1880', they suggest, 'the Empire was probably a snare and a delusion – a flame not worth the candle.'[29] In addition, they argue that the empire required subsidies, the most important of which were in the field of defence, necessitating the maintenance of artificially high levels of taxation in Britain. On the one hand, if the empire had made a fair contribution to imperial defence, taxes in Britain might have been reduced by 20 per cent. On the other, if Britain had relinquished empire and spent as much on defence as France and Germany, taxes would have fallen by some 12 per cent. Concluding their study, Davis and Huttenback state: 'The British as a whole did not benefit economically from the Empire.'[30] Their interpretation, however, can be criticised in a number of ways.[31]

Avner Offer suggests that Davis and Huttenback have overestimated British defence expenditure and underestimated that of other comparable powers, especially France. Offer's figures indicate that far from spending more than France, Britain spent about a third less on defence. Focusing on India, Offer

"NEW CROWNS FOR OLD ONES!"

(ALADDIN *adapted.*)

A cartoon from *Punch* drawn by Sir John Tenniel in 1876 depicting the prime minister, Benjamin Disraeli, crowning Queen Victoria Empress of India. Evaluate the representation of the queen and Disraeli in this cartoon.

shows that by paying for British and Indian troops serving overseas, India actually subsidised Britain. Andrew Porter, moreover, has suggested that much of the defence spending cited by Davis and Huttenback, far from representing an imperial subsidy, reflected Britain's position as a world-wide trading nation. Porter also accuses Davis and Huttenback of neglecting the empire's value as a supplier of low-cost commodities (foodstuffs and raw materials) to Britain. A. G. Hopkins, furthermore, criticises Davis and Huttenback's concentration on formal, constitutional empire, at the expense of informal empire. Focusing on Davis and Huttenback's historical methods, Hopkins also questions whether the consequences of imperialism can ever be assessed by accounting procedures alone. Indeed, Davis and Huttenback disregard other, non-quantifiable, benefits of empire such as international prestige, feelings of security, and the spread of British 'civilisation' and culture. On this final question, it can be suggested that the cultural exchange was a reciprocal process.

Imperial Britain

From the late nineteenth century, the growth of an 'imperial nationalism' can be identified. The new-found reverence for empire coalesced around monarchism, militarism and notions of racial superiority, or Social Darwinism. Between the death of her husband, Prince Albert, in 1861 and her re-emergence into public life 15 years later, Queen Victoria was a remote, even unpopular figure. Her elevation in 1876 to the position of Empress of India marked her transformation in the public mind from 'petulant widow to imperial matriarch'.[32] Indeed, the monarchy became increasingly associated with imperial imagery. This reached a remarkable climax when representatives from throughout the empire came to London in 1897 to celebrate Victoria's diamond jubilee. The second half of the nineteenth century also witnessed a growth in popularity of the armed forces, with military figures such as General Gordon, killed at Khartoum in 1885, raised to the status of national heroes. The depiction of such figures as representatives of a master people fuelled notions of racial superiority.

Imperial nationalism was reflected in juvenile literature, advertising, theatre, youth organisations and the educational system. The new enthusiasm for empire, moreover, was not confined to any one class in society. Such diverse institutions as public schools and working men's clubs demonstrated patriotic pride in empire. To what extent has imperial nationalism survived to the present day?

Document case study

7.1 Memorandum by William Gladstone (colonial secretary), 18 June 1846

The multiplication of colonies at the other end of the world must at all times be a matter of serious consideration; but especially at a time when we have already land almost infinite to defend that we cannot occupy, people to reduce to order whom we have not been able to keep in friendly relations, and questions in so many departments of government to manage, the discussion of which has been found embarrassing at home, and which appear to be thought fully equal in the demands they make to any energies that Executive Government is able to apply to them.

Source: Public Record Office, London, CO 144/1

7.2 Letter from Lord Clarendon (foreign secretary) to Sir Thomas Wade (Her Majesty's minister in Peking), 7 April 1870

British interests in China are strictly commercial, or, at all events, only so far political as they may be for the protection of commerce and of British subjects in their lawful pursuits. The British Government have neither the desire nor the intention to interfere with the internal administration of China, neither do they wish to employ any other action than that of friendly representation upon the Imperial Government for the defence of British subjects or for the redress of wrongs done to them.

Source: Nathan A. Pelcovits, *Old China hands and the Foreign Office*, New York, 1948, p. 85

7.3 Memorandum by Lord Palmerston (foreign secretary), 29 September 1850

These half civilised governments, such as those of China, Portugal, Spanish America, require a dressing every eight or ten years to keep them in order. Their minds are too shallow to receive an impression that will last longer than some such period, and warning is of little use. They care little for words and they must not only see the stick but actually feel it on their shoulders before they yield to that only argument which to them brings conviction, the *argumentum Baculinum* [argument of the stick].

Source: Ronald Hyam, *Britain's imperial century, 1815–1914*, 2nd edn, Basingstoke, 1993, p. 119

7.4 Speech by Sir Charles Dilke (under-secretary of state for foreign affairs), 25 July 1882

Egypt forms our highway to India and to the East generally . . . As regards the Suez Canal, England has a double interest; it has a predominant commercial interest, because 82 per cent of the trade passing through the Canal is British trade, and it has a predominant political interest caused by the fact that the Canal is the principal highway to India, Ceylon, the Straits and British Burmah, where 250,000,000 live under our rule; and also to China where we have vast interests and 84 per cent of the external trade of that still more enormous Empire. It is also one of the roads to our Colonial Empire in Australia and New Zealand.

Source: *Hansard's parliamentary debates, Commons*, vol. 272, col. 1720

7.5 *Pall Mall Gazette*, 4 February 1884

In times past . . . we did what we pleased, where we pleased, and as we pleased. The whole of heathendom, to use a comprehensive term, was our inheritance, and the salt sea our peculiar possession. All that has changed. Europe has overflowed into Africa, Asia, America, Australasia and the Pacific. At every turn we are confronted with gunboats, the sea lairs, or the colonies of jealous and eager rivals . . . The world is filling up around us . . . Europe, no longer distracted by intestine [domestic] feuds, throws off ever increasing swarms to settle in other continents, and whereas, since Trafalgar, the Englishman has never found himself confronted by any other opponent but the savage with his spear, or the pirate in his prah, we now find every ocean highway furrowed by European ironclads, while over many a colonial frontier frowns the cannon of Continental rivals.

Source: Bernard Porter, *The lion's share: a short history of British imperialism*, 3rd edn, London, 1996, p. 117

7.6 Hobson and surplus capital

It is not too much to say that the modern foreign policy of Great Britain has been primarily a struggle for profitable markets of investment. To a larger extent every year Great Britain has been becoming a nation living upon tribute from abroad, and the classes who enjoy this tribute have had an ever-increasing incentive to employ the public policy, the public purse, and the public force to extend the field of their private investments, and to safeguard and improve their existing investments. This is, perhaps, the most important fact in modern politics, and the obscurity in which it is wrapped has constituted the gravest danger to our State . . .

It is this economic condition of affairs that forms the taproot of Imperialism. If the consuming public in this country raised its standard of consumption to keep pace with every rise of productive powers, there could be no excess of goods or capital clamorous to use Imperialism in order to find markets . . .

. . . It is not industrial progress that demands the opening up of new markets and areas of investment, but mal-distribution of consuming power which prevents the absorption of commodities and capital within the country.

Source: J. A. Hobson, *Imperialism: a study*, 3rd edn, London, 1938, pp. 53–54, 81, 85

Document case-study questions

1 What does 7.1 tell us about British attitudes towards imperial expansion?

2 How convincing do you find the claims made by Lord Clarendon in 7.2?

3 Compare the assessment of Britain's freedom of action in 7.3 with that of 7.5.

4 In what ways could 7.4 be used to support the strategic interpretation of Britain's occupation of Egypt?

5 How persuasive do you find J. A. Hobson's explanation for imperialism in 7.6?

Notes and references

1 Ronald Hyam, *Britain's imperial century, 1815–1914*, 2nd edn, Basingstoke, 1993, p. 30.

2 Oliver MacDonagh, 'The anti-imperialism of free trade', *Economic History Review*, vol. 14 (1962): 496.

3 John Gallagher and Ronald Robinson, 'The imperialism of free trade', *Economic History Review*, vol. 6 (1953): 11.

4 Gallagher and Robinson, 'Imperialism of free trade', p. 1.

5 Gallagher and Robinson, 'Imperialism of free trade', p. 9.

6 Gallagher and Robinson, 'Imperialism of free trade', p. 8.

7 Gallagher and Robinson, 'Imperialism of free trade', p. 13.

8 D. C. M. Platt, *Finance, trade, and politics in British foreign policy, 1815–1914*, Oxford, 1968, p. 316.

9 D. C. M. Platt, 'Further objections to an "imperialism of free trade", 1830–60', *Economic History Review*, vol. 26 (1973).

10 Rory Miller, *Britain and Latin America in the nineteenth and twentieth centuries*, London, 1993, pp. 54–58.

11 Gallagher and Robinson, 'Imperialism of free trade', p. 5.

12 Miller, *Britain and Latin America*, p. 41.

13 See Britten Dean, 'British informal empire: the case of China', *Journal of Commonwealth and Comparative Politics*, vol. 14 (1976).

14 Hyam, *Britain's imperial century*, pp. 130–31.

15 P. J. Cain and A. G. Hopkins, *British imperialism: innovation and expansion, 1688–1914*, London, 1993, pp. 313–14.

16 P. J. Cain and A. J. Hopkins, 'Gentlemanly capitalism and British expansion overseas. II: New imperialism, 1850–1945', *Economic History Review*, vol. 40 (1987): 11.

17 See D. K. Fieldhouse, '"Imperialism": an historiographical revision', *Economic History Review*, vol. 14 (1961).

18 Cain and Hopkins, 'New imperialism', p. 17.

19 Cain and Hopkins, *British imperialism*, p. 19.

20 Cain and Hopkins, 'New imperialism', p. 6.

21 Cain and Hopkins, *British imperialism*, p. 369.

22 See Andrew Porter, '"Gentlemanly capitalism" and empire: the British experience since 1750?', *Journal of Imperial Commonwealth History*, vol. 18 (1990); David Cannadine, 'Review article: the empire strikes back', *Past and Present*, vol. 147 (1995); D. K. Fieldhouse, 'Gentlemen, capitalists, and the British empire', *Journal of Imperial and Commonwealth History*, vol. 22 (1994).

23 Ronald Robinson and John Gallagher, 'The partition of Africa', in F. H. Hinsley (ed.), *The new Cambridge modern history: volume 11: material progress and world-wide problems, 1870–1898*, Cambridge, 1962, p. 594.

24 Robinson and Gallagher, 'The partition of Africa', p. 599.

25 Ronald Robinson and John Gallagher, *Africa and the Victorians: the official mind of imperialism*, 2nd edn, Basingstoke, 1981, p. 465.

26 See G. N. Sanderson, 'The European partition of Africa: coincidence or conjuncture?', *Journal of Imperial and Commonwealth History*, vol. 3 (1974).

27 A. G. Hopkins, 'The Victorians and Africa: a reconsideration of the occupation of Egypt, 1882', *Journal of African History*, vol. 27 (1986): 389.

28 See Nicholas Tarling, 'The establishment of the colonial régimes', in Nicholas Tarling (ed.), *The Cambridge history of South-East Asia*, vol. 2, Cambridge, 1992.

29 Lance E. Davis and Robert A. Huttenback, *Mammon and the pursuit of empire: the political economy of British imperialism, 1860–1912*, Cambridge, 1986, p. 110.

30 Davis and Huttenback, *Mammon and the pursuit of empire*, p. 306.

31 Avner Offer, 'The British Empire, 1870–1914: a waste of money?', *Economic History Review*, vol. 46 (1993); Andrew Porter, 'The balance sheet of empire, 1850–1914', *Historical Journal*, vol. 31 (1988); A. G. Hopkins, 'Accounting for the British Empire', *Journal of Imperial and Commonwealth History*, vol. 16 (1988).

32 John M. MacKenzie, *Propaganda and empire: the manipulation of British public opinion, 1880–1960*, Manchester, 1984, p. 4.

8 Challenges to imperial authority: South Africa and Ireland

Key dates

1795–1803 First period of British rule at the Cape
1798 Great Rising in Ireland
1801 Act of Union
1814 Cession of the Cape to Britain
1835–36 Annexation and retrocession of Queen Adelaide Province
1836 The Great Trek begins
1843 Annexation of Natal
1848 Annexation of Orange River Sovereignty
1854 Bloemfontein Convention
1877 Annexation of the Transvaal
1879–82 Irish Land War
1881 Battle of Majuba
Pretoria Convention
1886 Discovery of gold at Witwatersrand
1895 Jameson Raid
1899 Bloemfontein Conference
1899–1902 South African War
1902 Treaty of Vereeniging
1910 Unification of South Africa
1916 Easter Rising
1919–21 Anglo-Irish War
1921 Anglo-Irish Treaty
1922–23 Irish Civil War

Sporadic resistance to imperial power was a characteristic feature of Britain's nineteenth-century empire. South Africa and Ireland, however, represented persistent threats to imperial authority which Britain proved incapable of subduing. In both territories, the problems confronting Britain stemmed from the existence of peoples – Boers in South Africa and nationalists in Ireland – whose determination to preserve their distinct cultures was matched by their fierce opposition to subordination to Britain. To make matters worse for the British, nationalists in Ireland and Boers in South Africa sympathised with each other's quest for separation from Britain. While both territories were nominally encompassed within the structures of the British Empire in the early decades of the twentieth century, neither proved comfortable companions for Britain, Ireland leaving the Commonwealth in 1949, South Africa following 12 years later.

South Africa

The British and the Boers

A group of Dutchmen, who had been forced to winter in Table Bay just to the north of the Cape of Good Hope after losing their ship off the South African coast, recommended in 1649 that the Dutch East India Company occupy the area. The Company directors were persuaded and three years later dispatched Jan van Riebeeck with instructions to construct a fort and supply Dutch fleets passing to and from the East. Despite the limited objectives of the Company, the settlement began to grow in terms of both area and population. By 1707, when the Company ceased to provide free passage for Europeans, there were around 700 Company servants in addition to a settler community of 2,000. The settled area, moreover, had begun to stretch far inland, often at the expense of local pastoralists (cattle farmers), the Khoi, whom the settlers called Hottentots. A further ominous development was the arrival in 1658 of the first ship-load of slaves. From this time on, the Cape became a slave-owning society. In the final years of the eighteenth century, conflicts in Europe which spilled over into the non-European world were to have a profound and lasting effect on the history of South Africa.

To prevent the strategically important Cape region from falling into the hands of France, Britain occupied the region in 1795. Although the Dutch regained the Cape under the terms of the Treaty of Amiens in 1803, three years later Britain once more took the Cape following the resumption of war with France. British possession of the area was recognised in the peace settlement of 1814. Without any form of consultation, therefore, the Dutch farmers of the Cape, whom the British termed Boers, found themselves under British sovereignty. Minor rebellions in 1799 and 1801 were a foretaste of the tension which was to characterise relations between Britain and the Boers throughout the nineteenth century.

Culturally, the Boers exhibited many features which marked them out from the British. Being derived from the original settlers, the Boers spoke a simplified form of Dutch, known as Afrikaans. Strong adherents to Calvinism, the Boers developed a powerful sense of identity and racial superiority which was used to justify their dominance over black Africans. British attitudes, by contrast, were being influenced more and more by the missionary-philanthropic movement which was finding favour in Britain in the early decades of the nineteenth century (see Chapter 4). In consequence, there was a clash of concepts over the correct treatment of black Africans. Early differences were exposed by the introduction of the 'Black Circuit' in 1811–12.

The Black Circuit was a circuit court which was charged with enquiring into complaints of mistreatment by employers of their non-white servants. Not surprisingly, it was greeted with a mixture of indignation and incredulity by the frontier settlers. Apart from striking at the heart of their notions of racial superiority, the circuit also weakened farmers' authority over their servants. Indignation turned to violence in 1815, when an uprising broke out which was only extinguished with the use of force. The Cape government's Fiftieth Ordinance, which provided the Hottentots with equality before the law (see Chapter 4), aroused a similar degree of resentment among the settlers. The abolition of slavery throughout the British Empire in 1833 hardened attitudes still further, not least since the many former slave-owners were dissatisfied with the level of compensation provided by the British government. However, the decisive split came in 1836 with the retrocession of the Queen Adelaide Province.

In May 1835, Governor Benjamin D'Urban had annexed the fertile area between the Kei and Fish rivers along the east coast of the Cape. As the indigenous farming people, the Xhosa, began to be driven from their land, missionary objections found a receptive audience in Britain, where a parliamentary select committee on Aborigines was meeting. In 1836, D'Urban was instructed by the Colonial Secretary, Lord Glenelg, to reverse the annexation of Queen Adelaide Province. With their hopes of settler advance along the well-watered eastern corridor dashed, the Boers began to trek away from Cape Colony in the final months of 1836, travelling northwards across the Orange River to the 'empty lands' which their reconnaissance parties had talked of. By 1840, six thousand Boers had migrated in what became known as the Great Trek.

Although in some senses the Great Trek can be seen as part of the long process of white expansion, it did contain some distinct features. Whereas in the past settlers had migrated, expecting the frontier to follow them, those who embarked on the Great Trek did so with the intention of escaping from British authority. The Boer leader Piet Retief spoke for his people when he expressed the hope that the British government would 'allow us to govern ourselves without its interference in future'.[1] As if to highlight the new departure, those who participated in the Great Trek became known as voortrekkers, or pioneers. Disagreements over the direction to be taken by the Trek, nevertheless, precipitated a division in the voortrekker community, the majority settling in Natal under Retief's leadership, the remainder pushing on beyond the Vaal River.

The Great Trek presented Britain with a dilemma. On the one hand, a mixture of self-interest and genuine concern for the welfare of black Africans dictated that Britain should extend her authority over the new areas occupied by the Boer communities. On the other, British governments blanched at the potential costs of assuming new responsibilities. A policy of expansion in the 1840s gave way to one of abandonment in the early 1850s.

In May 1842, British troops occupied Port Natal, and the territory was annexed the following year. Acting on his own authority and out of concern for the security and stability of the Cape frontiers, Governor Sir Harry Smith annexed the area between the Vaal and Orange rivers, known as the Orange River

Sovereignty, in 1848. Smith's successor, Sir George Cathcart, however, gave his political masters in London the sobering news that to rule the Sovereignty effectively would require a permanent garrison of two thousand men as well as a greatly increased civil establishment. Taking this warning to heart, the British government abandoned the Orange River Sovereignty, which thereafter became known as the Orange Free State, under the terms of the Bloemfontein Convention of February 1854. Two years earlier, Britain had renounced all claims to authority over the region north of the Vaal River known as the Transvaal.

Sir George Grey, who succeeded Cathcart in 1854, had opposed the policy of withdrawal and in 1858 recommended bringing the Europeans in southern Africa back under British control through a federation. The Colonial Office, concerned about the potential costs of such a scheme, rejected his recommendation. It was not until the 1870s that the federal idea was revived. Lord Carnarvon, who became colonial secretary in 1874, was a strong adherent of federation in southern Africa. Far from being a drain on the British exchequer, he argued, 'Federation would greatly improve and cheapen the administration of affairs in almost every branch and greatly lessen the probability of a demand for aid in the shape of Imperial money or troops.'[2] As a prelude, he hoped, to its incorporation into a South African federation, Carnarvon approved the annexation of the Transvaal on 12 April 1877. This action, however, merely provoked an armed rising among Boers which culminated in the defeat of a British force at Majuba in February 1881. The new Liberal government of William Gladstone, plagued by troubles in Ireland and anxious to avoid a similarly tortured situation in South Africa, favoured conciliation. At the Pretoria Convention in August 1881, it recognised the Transvaal's 'complete self-government, subject to the Suzerainty

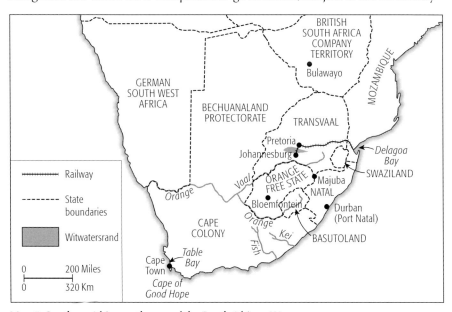

Map 5. Southern Africa on the eve of the South African War

of Her Majesty'. Three years later the Pretoria agreement was superseded by the London Convention, which made no mention of suzerainty. The discovery of vast gold reserves at Witwatersrand (see Map 5) in 1886 allowed the Transvaal to maintain its new-found political independence from a position of economic strength.

By the end of the nineteenth century, the Transvaal had become the world's major supplier of gold, producing over 25 per cent of total output. Not surprisingly, the Transvaal began to replace the Cape as the economic centre of South Africa (see document 8.1). The discovery of gold also had a profound effect on the social composition of the Transvaal. The lure of gold attracted male workers, who became known as 'Uitlanders', from Britain, continental Europe, and from further afield. Totalling 44,000 by 1896, the Uitlanders outnumbered Boer males in the Transvaal. In an effort to maintain the Boer character of the Transvaal, the Boers discriminated against the Uitlanders, denying them voting and citizenship rights. It was the question of Uitlander rights which precipitated the breakdown in relations between Britain and the Transvaal, culminating in the South African War of 1899–1902. The extent to which the war had deeper causes is a question which has exercised historians since the early twentieth century.

The South African War and the historians

Whilst he was in South Africa in 1899 as correspondent for the *Manchester Guardian*, J. A. Hobson developed his enduringly influential explanation for the outbreak of hostilities, which he published a year later as *The war in South Africa: its causes and effects*. In his opinion, capitalists and mine-owners were to blame for the war. Resentful of the erosion of their profits resulting from additional charges placed on their operations by the Transvaal government of President Paul Kruger, the mine-owners sought to replace it with one that would be more responsive to their needs. Having failed in December 1895 to overthrow the Kruger government in a *coup d'état*, known as the Jameson Raid, they provoked full-scale war between Britain and the Transvaal in 1899.

While rejecting the conspiratorial elements of Hobson's interpretation, P. J. Cain and A. G. Hopkins have reiterated the central importance which Hobson ascribed to economic considerations in the outbreak of war. First, they stress the scale of Britain's financial stake in South Africa. Not only was over half of the £74 million invested in gold mining British, but also by 1900 Britain had captured two-thirds of South Africa's rapidly expanding import trade. In consequence, Cain and Hopkins argue that 'the costly decision to bring the Boer republics under control can only be understood in the context of the need to defend Britain's substantial financial and commercial stake in South Africa'.[3] A related economic interpretation suggests that Britain went to war to secure physical control of the gold mines, not merely in the interests of sustaining her pre-eminence in the world's financial markets, but also because of her relatively low gold reserves.[4] Beyond economic explanations, the role of prominent person-alities has had an enduring appeal. The two individuals who have traditionally borne most of the blame for the outbreak of war have been the colonial secretary,

Joseph Chamberlain, and the high commissioner in South Africa, Sir Alfred Milner.

Interpretations which focus either on economic considerations or on the role of personalities are unsatisfactory for a number of reasons. First, Hobson, and those who have followed his line of reasoning, exaggerate the influence of the mine-owners: divided among themselves, they studiously avoided taking the political initiative following the disastrous Jameson Raid in 1895. Far from favouring war, which threatened the suspension of mine operations, with potentially crippling losses, the mine-owners pursued the much more limited objective of promoting reforms within the Transvaal administration. Moreover, while South Africa was Britain's largest single market on the African continent, it still played a fairly insignificant role in Britain's export trade, just £15 million a year at the end of the nineteenth century. It would be stretching credibility to suggest that Britain embarked on a war which eventually cost over £200 million

SWAIN SC

"DOGS OF WAR."

Oom Paul. "MAY I ASK IF THOSE DOGS ARE INTENDED FOR ANY SPECIAL PURPOSE?"
J-E Ch-mb-rl-n. "WELL, GUV'NOR, THAT'S AS MAY BE! MERELY GIVIN' 'EM A LITTLE GENTLE EXERCISE!"

A cartoon produced in 1899 for *Punch* shows the president of the Transvaal, Paul Kruger, quizzing the colonial secretary, Joseph Chamberlain, about his intentions. Is this a fair and accurate portrayal of Joseph Chamberlain's role in the outbreak of the South African War?

to protect her share of the South African market. So far as gold is concerned, contemporary records reveal no anxiety on the part of Britain about either the gold supply to London or the low level of her gold reserves. Referring to access to South Africa's gold, moreover, Iain R. Smith has convincingly argued that 'the British government had no more need to annex the gold-rich territory of the Transvaal to secure this than it did to annex those areas of the Yukon, California or Australia where gold was also being mined at this time'.[5] Focusing on the role of particular personalities is equally unsatisfactory.

As regards Chamberlain, Andrew Porter has conclusively demonstrated that he neither pushed a reluctant cabinet into a policy of confrontation with the Transvaal, nor dominated the ageing premier, Lord Salisbury, on South African questions.[6] A better case can be made for seeing Milner as responsible for war. Once the resort to war had been made, he freely admitted: 'I precipitated the crisis, which was inevitable, before it was too late.'[7] By manipulating the press in both South Africa and Britain, Milner created a climate of opinion which made compromise difficult.[8] Furthermore, it was Milner's abrupt termination in early June 1899 of the Bloemfontein Conference, which had been established to discuss the divisive issue of Uitlander voting rights, which shattered Boer confidence in British good faith, leading to the outbreak of war in October. Nevertheless, in pursuing the objective of upholding British supremacy in southern Africa, Milner was at one with the British cabinet. Indeed, by 1899 Salisbury, Chamberlain and the rest of their cabinet colleagues agreed on the necessity of direct intervention if South Africa were to be retained for the empire. As Lord Salisbury put it: 'the real point to be made good to South Africa is that we not the Dutch are Boss'.[9]

It was the discovery of gold at Witwatersrand in 1886 which altered the geopolitical complexion of South Africa. Not only did the economic balance of power shift from the Cape to the Transvaal, but also the Boers possessed for the first time the financial strength to make their independence from Britain a reality. In the hope of encircling the Transvaal and discovering new mineral deposits to the north, the British government gave a royal charter to the South Africa Company of millionaire businessman Cecil Rhodes. By the mid-1890s, however, the policy of encirclement lay in ruins. Not only did Rhodes' South Africa Company fail to find mineral wealth, but also the opening in 1894 of the railway linking Delagoa Bay in Portuguese Mozambique to Witwatersrand meant that the Transvaal, for the first time, possessed a route to the sea which avoided British territory.

In the later 1890s, British statesmen focused on the Uitlander rights since they seemed to present the best means of effecting a transfer of power in the Transvaal from the Boers to pro-British elements. The significance of the Uitlander question was not lost on the Boers. As Kruger emphasised at the Bloemfontein Conference, 'to grant the franchise to any large number of aliens would immediately result in the outvoting of the old burghers [farmers]'.[10] It was Boer preparedness to fight on this issue which led to armed conflict. Three years of bitter warfare followed, the latter stages of which were characterised by a prolonged guerrilla campaign waged by Boer commandos.

War, reconciliation and secession

In an attempt to extinguish Boer resistance, the commander-in-chief of British forces, Lord Kitchener, adopted a scorched-earth policy, burning Boer crops and farmsteads, and removing Boer civilians to concentration camps, where some 28,000, mostly women and children, perished. Worn down by a war of attrition, the Boers capitulated in May 1902. The subsequent Treaty of Vereeniging, nevertheless, included one significant concession to the Boers: the enfranchisement of non-whites in the former Boer republics was made dependent on the consent of the white population. Counting on the English-speakers to uphold British interests, the Liberal government of Sir Henry Campbell-Bannerman decided in February 1906 to grant internal self-government to the Transvaal. Divisions within the English-speaking community, however, allowed the Boer party, Het Volk, to prevail in the first elections a year later, prompting Milner to observe that Britain had 'given South Africa back to the Boers'.[11] A similar pattern was repeated in the Orange River Colony (the former Orange Free State), where elections were held in 1908. Over the next two years discussions took place aimed at unifying the territories of South Africa. On 31 May 1910, exactly eight years after surrendering to the British, the Boer leader, Louis Botha, became prime minister of the Union of South Africa. Although the new dominion supported Britain through two world wars, Anglo-Boer suspicion was never completely erased. In the wake of growing criticism of its racial policies, known as apartheid, South Africa withdrew from the Commonwealth in 1961. The ending of apartheid, and the election of Nelson Mandela as South Africa's first black president, facilitated South Africa's re-entry into the Commonwealth 33 years later.

Ireland

The Irish question

'My belief', wrote the South African prime minister, J. C. Smuts, in August 1921, 'is that Ireland is travelling the same painful road as South Africa, and is destined to achieve the same success.'[12] As these comments suggest, the modern history of Ireland and South Africa exhibit many parallels. Drawn firmly within the British Empire at the beginning of the nineteenth century against the will of large sections of the population, both fought wars in the early twentieth century to free themselves from imperial control. While Britain managed to maintain links with Ireland and South Africa through the structures of the Commonwealth, they were in many ways restless dominions, both departing from that organisation within 16 years of the end of the Second World War.

Exploiting Britain's preoccupation with revolutionary France, Irish nationalists tried to seize power in the so-called Great Rising of 1798. These events convinced British statesmen that the security threat posed by Ireland could only be neutralised by a full union between Britain and Ireland, which was effected by the Act of Union on 1 January 1801. The union, however, was an unhappy one.

Most Catholics, who formed the largest community in Ireland, came to favour home rule. In the 1870s, the Irish Parliamentary Party (IPP) emerged from the Home Rule League, which had been established in 1873. In the 1885 general election, the IPP won 85 seats. The predominantly Protestant province of Ulster, nevertheless, was opposed to home rule, favouring instead continuing union with Britain. Violence was never far from the surface. Between 1879 and 1882 the National League, a mass nationalist organisation associated with the IPP, conducted the so-called Land War, a campaign of rent strikes, boycotts and intimidation of landlords. The strong strain of physical force nationalism in Ireland was brutally demonstrated in 1882 when the new chief secretary for Ireland, Lord Frederick Cavendish, was assassinated by a group calling themselves the Irish National Invincibles.

In an attempt to defuse the mounting problems in Ireland, the Liberal prime minister, W. E. Gladstone, sponsored two home-rule bills in 1886 and 1893, neither of which reached the statute book. As attention switched to the growing problems in South Africa, Irish nationalists began to sympathise openly with Boer resistance to British imperial control. Arthur Griffith, who visited the Transvaal in the 1890s, was encouraged by the anti-British atmosphere which confirmed to him that 'God Almighty had not made the earth for the sole use of the Anglo-Saxon race'.[13] The outbreak of the South African War in 1899 energised the Irish nationalist movement. Griffith's newspaper, the *United Irishman*, carried pro-Boer articles, while in October the Irish Transvaal Committee was formed to support the Boer republics and dissuade Irishmen from enlisting in the British army. Griffith, who was one of the Committee's chief activists, went on to found the Irish nationalist organisation Sinn Fein in 1905. The activities of two Irish Transvaal brigades, which had been formed in 1899 and 1900 to fight for the Boer republics, also filled Irish nationalists with pride. Maud Gonne, a leading figure on the Irish Transvaal Committee, argued that the brigades 'had done more for Ireland's honour than all of us at home'.[14]

Despite the new impetus given to Irish nationalism by the South African War, progress towards home rule was slow. It was not until 1910 that the Liberal government, reliant on the support of Irish MPs following its poor showing in the 1910 general election, turned its attention once more to the question. A third home-rule bill, unlike its two predecessors, reached the statute book in the early days of the First World War. The 1914 Home Rule Act, however, was not to be implemented until after the war and contained a proviso that amending legislation would be passed to cater for Ulster. As the war dragged on without end in sight, nationalist impatience manifested itself in the Easter Rising of 1916. On 24 April 1916, a group of nationalists seized the General Post Office in Dublin, proclaiming an Irish republic. Swift British reprisals, including the execution of the rising's ringleaders, merely succeeded in increasing support for nationalist organisations. Despite having little to do with the 1916 rising, Sinn Fein was the major beneficiary. In the December 1918 general election, Sinn Fein captured 73 Irish seats compared with the IPP's paltry 6. Refusing to take up their seats at Westminster, the Sinn Feiners not only set themselves up as an Irish parliament but also issued a declaration of independence in January 1919. Almost immediately, an Anglo-Irish war broke out which was characterised by atrocities on both sides.

Ireland divided

Under the determined leadership of Michael Collins, the Irish Republican Army (IRA) demonstrated, as the Boer commandos had done twenty years earlier, that

THE KINDEST CUT OF ALL.

WELSH WIZARD. "I NOW PROCEED TO CUT THIS MAP INTO TWO PARTS AND PLACE THEM IN THE HAT. AFTER A SUITABLE INTERVAL THEY WILL BE FOUND TO HAVE COME TOGETHER OF THEIR OWN ACCORD—(ASIDE)—AT LEAST LET'S HOPE SO; I'VE NEVER DONE THIS TRICK BEFORE."

A *Punch* cartoon shows the British prime minister, Lloyd George, unveiling his doomed 1920 Government of Ireland Act. What point do you think the cartoonist is trying to make?

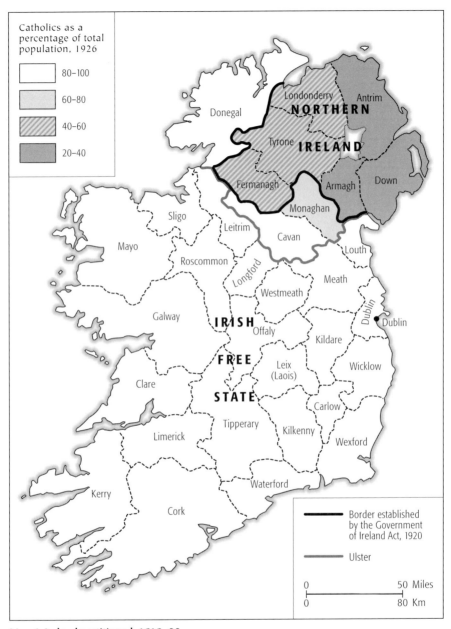

Map 6. Ireland partitioned, 1919–22

a comparatively small, but strongly motivated, irregular force could frustrate much larger British forces. Prime minister David Lloyd George's attempt to end the war through the 1920 Government of Ireland Act, which created two home-rule parliaments plus a council of Ireland composed of representatives from both legislatures, proved a failure (see cartoon on p. 93). By mid-1921, the military commander in Ireland, General Nevil Macready, was warning that the suppression of the Irish rebels would necessitate 'an operation of war more extensive and more bitter than would be acceptable to the judgement and conscience of the British people'.[15] With such considerations in mind, Lloyd George approved a truce in July 1921. In October, an Irish delegation, led by Collins and Griffith, arrived in London. Following nearly two months of complex negotiations, an agreement was reached under which Ireland would be partitioned, the new Irish Free State becoming a dominion under royal sovereignty. (See Map 6.) Ireland was also bound to take over a portion of the national debt and permit Royal Navy access to three treaty ports.

In January 1922, the Anglo-Irish Treaty was narrowly ratified by the Irish parliament. Appalled by continuing royal sovereignty and the partition of Ireland, the president of the Irish republic, Eamon de Valera, promptly resigned. By June 1922, divisions over the Anglo-Irish Treaty had spilled over into violence. The occupation of the Four Courts building in Dublin by members of the IRA marked the start of the Irish Civil War. Despite the deaths of Collins and Griffith in August, the pro-treaty elements had prevailed by May 1923. De Valera, however, returned to prominence when his Fianna Fail party came to power in 1932. Determined to sever the ties with Britain, he declared the Free State a sovereign state in 1937 and a year later induced the British to relinquish their naval bases on Irish soil. In 1949, the awkward fiction of Ireland's Commonwealth member-ship was brought to an end. To what extent have ingrained tensions between Protestants and Catholics in Ulster continued to bedevil Anglo-Irish relations?

Document case study

8.1 Memorandum by Lord Selborne (parliamentary under-secretary for colonies), 26 March 1896

[T]he key to the future of South Africa is in the Transvaal. It is the richest spot on earth. The only properly speaking populous spots in South Africa are already within it; and while the population of Cape Colony, of Natal, of Rhodesia etc. will increase but slowly and gradually, the population of the Transvaal has increased, and will continue to increase, by leaps and bounds, and in fifty years time will probably be reckoned in millions.

My postulate therefore is that the Transvaal is going to be by far the richest, by far the most populous part of South Africa, that it is going to be the natural capital state and centre of South African commercial, social and political life.

Source: Ronald Robinson and John Gallagher, *Africa and the Victorians: the official mind of imperialism*, 2nd edn, London, 1981, p. 434

8.2 Letter from Sir Alfred Milner to Joseph Chamberlain, 23 February 1898

There is no way out of the political troubles of S. Africa except reform in the Transvaal or war. And at present the chances of reform in the Transvaal are worse than ever . . . In their determination to keep all power in their own hands and to use it with a total disregard of the interests of the unenfranchised, as well as in their own hatred of Great Britain, the vast majority of them [the Boers] are firmly united.

Source: Cecil Headlam (ed.), *The Milner papers: South Africa, 1897–1899*, London, 1931, p. 221

8.3 Telegram from Milner to Chamberlain, 4 May 1899

The spectacle of thousands of British subjects kept permanently in the position of helots, constantly chafing under undoubted grievances, and calling vainly to Her Majesty's Government for redress, does steadily undermine the influence and reputation of Great Britain and the respect for the British Government within its own dominions.

Source: Cecil Headlam (ed.), *The Milner papers: South Africa, 1897–1899*, London, 1931, p. 353

8.4 Letter from Chamberlain to Milner, 2 September 1899

It is a great thing to say that the majority of the people have, as I believe, recognised that there is a greater issue than the franchise or the grievances of the Uitlanders at stake, and that our supremacy in S. Africa and our existence as a great Power in the world are involved in the result of our present controversy.

Source: Cecil Headlam (ed.), *The Milner papers: South Africa, 1897–1899*, London, 1931, p. 526

8.5 Hobson's explanation for the South African War

The men who, owning the South African press and political organisations, engineered the agitation which has issued in this war, are the same men whose pockets will swell with this increase; open-eyed and persistent they have pursued their course, plunging South Africa into a temporary ruin in order that they may emerge victorious, a small confederacy of international mine-owners and speculators holding the treasures of South Africa in the hollow of their hands.

Source: J. A. Hobson, *The war in South Africa: its causes and effects*, 2nd edn, London, 1900, p. 240

8.6 'Memoirs of the Boer War', unfinished manuscript written by J. C. Smuts between 1903 and 1906

Smuts had been state attorney in Paul Kruger's government, and subsequently served as prime minister of South Africa on two separate occasions, 1919–24 and 1939–48.

It was the rooted conviction of the Boers generally, a conviction which was I believe shared by their more responsible leaders, that the war was at bottom a mine-owners' war, that it had its origin in the Jameson Raid – in the firm resolve of the mine-owners to get the political control of the Transvaal into their hands by fair means or foul, to shape the legislation and administration of the country along lines dictated by their economic interests, and to destroy the Boer Government which had stupidly proved obdurate to their threats no less than to their seductions.

Source: W. K. Hancock and Jean van der Poel (eds.), *Selections from the Smuts papers*, vol. 1, London, 1966, p. 623

8.7 The *Sligo Champion*, 18 October 1899

The Sligo Champion *was one of the many nationalist newspapers in Ireland which supported the Boers.*

History does not record a more diabolical or more audacious scheme of plunder than that in which England is now engaged in South Africa . . . The sympathy of every just and upright man in the world will go forth to the brave Boers in their manly struggle for the preservation of their independence as a Nation . . . May God strengthen their arms and send them a speedy recovery from all reverses.

Source: Donal P. McCracken, *The Irish pro-Boers, 1877–1902*, Johannesburg, 1989, p. 51

8.8 Speech in the Commons by Lloyd George on the Anglo-Irish Treaty, 14 December 1921

On the British side we have allegiance to the Crown, partnership in the Empire, security of our shores, non-coercion of Ulster . . . On the Irish side there is the one supreme condition, that the Irish people as a nation should be free in their own land to work out their own national destinies in their own way. These two nations will, I believe, be reconciled.

Source: Frederick Madden and John Darwin (eds.), *The dominions and India since 1900*, Westport, 1993, p. 567

8.9 Speech by Arthur Griffith in the Irish parliament, 19 December 1921

I signed the Treaty not as an ideal thing, but fully believing, as I believe now, it is a Treaty honourable to Ireland, and safeguards the vital interests of Ireland . . . I ask the people of Ireland, and the Irish people everywhere, to ratify this Treaty, to end this bitter conflict of centuries, to end it forever, to take away that poison that has been rankling in the two countries and ruining the relationship of good neighbours.

Source: Frederick Madden and John Darwin (eds.), *The dominions and India since 1900*, Westport, 1993, pp. 568, 570

8.10 Speech by de Valera in the Irish parliament, 19 December 1921

I am against this treaty because it will not end the centuries of conflict between the two nations of Great Britain and Ireland. We went out [to the negotiations in London] to effect such a reconciliation and we have brought back a thing which will not even reconcile our own people much less reconcile Britain and Ireland.

Source: Frederick Madden and John Darwin (eds.), *The dominions and India since 1900*, Westport, 1993, p. 570

Document case-study questions

1 How could 8.1 and 8.4 be used to explain Britain's motives in going to war in South Africa?

2 What light do 8.2 and 8.3 shed on the question of Milner's responsiblity for the outbreak of the South African War?

3 Compare J. A. Hobson's explanation in 8.5 for the South African War with that of J. C. Smuts in 8.6.

4 Comment on the *Sligo Champion*'s reaction to the South African War in 8.7.

5 Compare the different reactions to the Anglo-Irish Treaty (1921) in 8.8, 8.9 and 8.10.

Notes and references

1 Leonard Thompson, *A history of South Africa*, New Haven, 1995, p. 88.

2 C. W. De Kiewiet, *A history of South Africa: social and economic*, London, 1966 (first published 1941), p. 101.

3 P. J. Cain and A. G. Hopkins, 'Gentlemanly capitalism and British overseas expansion. II: New imperialism, 1850–1945', *Economic History Review*, vol. 40 (1987): 13. See also P. J. Cain and A. G. Hopkins, *British imperialism: innovation and expansion, 1688–1914*, London, 1993, pp. 369–81.

4 See Shula Marks and Stanley Trapido, 'Lord Milner and the South African State', *History Workshop*, vol. 8 (1979): 50–80.

5 Iain R. Smith, *The origins of the South African War, 1899–1902*, London, 1996, p. 411.

6 See Andrew Porter, 'Lord Salisbury, Mr Chamberlain and South Africa, 1895–9', *Journal of Imperial and Commonwealth History*, vol. 1 (1972): 3–26.

7 Smith, *Origins*, p. 416.

8 See A. N. Porter, 'Sir Alfred Milner and the press, 1897–1899', *Historical Journal*, vol. 16 (1973): 323–39.

9 A. N. Porter, *The origins of the South African War: Joseph Chamberlain and the diplomacy of imperialism, 1895–99*, Manchester, 1980, p. 228.

10 Smith, *Origins*, p. 419.

11 Ronald Hyam, 'The myth of the "Magnanimous Gesture": the Liberal government, Smuts, and conciliation, 1906', in Ronald Hyam and Ged Martin (eds.), *Reappraisals in British imperial history*, London, 1975, p. 175.

12 Keith Jeffrey (ed.), *'An Irish empire?' Aspects of Ireland and the British Empire*, Manchester, 1996, p. 8.

13 Keith Jeffrey, 'The Irish military tradition and the British Empire', in Jeffrey, *'An Irish empire?'*, p. 95.

14 Donal P. McCracken, *The Irish pro-Boers, 1877–1902*, Johannesburg, 1989, p. 145.

15 Michael Hughes, *Ireland divided: the roots of the modern Irish problem*, Cardiff, 1994, p. 51.

9 The British Empire in the Middle East

Key dates

1915   Hussein–McMahon correspondence

1917   Balfour Declaration

1920   San Remo Conference

1922   Egyptian 'independence'

1936   Anglo-Egyptian Treaty

1937   Peel Commission

1939   White Paper on Palestine

1948   Britain abandons Palestine

1951   Nationalisation of Anglo-Iranian Oil

1956   Suez Crisis

1958   Britain dispatches troops to Jordan

1961   Britain dispatches troops to Kuwait

1971   Britain leaves the Persian Gulf

For much of the nineteenth century Britain had striven to prevent hostile European powers from encroaching on the Middle East, an area vital for the protection of her imperial interests in India and beyond. The principal method of achieving this had been the preservation of weak Ottoman (Turkish) rule in the region. From the late nineteenth century, however, the foundations of British policy were undermined by Turkey's increasing identification with Germany. The old certainties were finally shattered by her alignment with the Germans in the First World War. Turkey's defeat left Britain as the dominant power in the Middle East (see Map 7), a position which she maintained until the early 1950s. Despite her diplomatic defeat at the hands of Egypt in 1956, Britain maintained extensive Middle Eastern commitments for a further 15 years.

From Palestine mandate to Israeli state

Turkish lands in the Middle East were peopled largely by Arabs. The spread of Arab nationalism is often traced to the Turkish Revolution of 1908, which witnessed the coming to power of 'Young Turks' determined to assert the Turkish

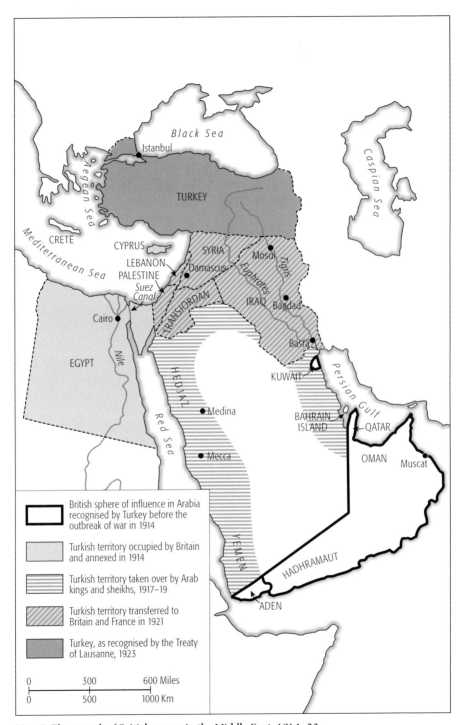

Map 7. The growth of British power in the Middle East, 1914–23

Legend:
- British sphere of influence in Arabia recognised by Turkey before the outbreak of war in 1914
- Turkish territory occupied by Britain and annexed in 1914
- Turkish territory taken over by Arab kings and sheikhs, 1917–19
- Turkish territory transferred to Britain and France in 1921
- Turkey, as recognised by the Treaty of Lausanne, 1923

Scale:
0 — 300 — 600 Miles
0 — 500 — 1000 Km

character of the empire. From this time Arabs began to look to break free from Turkish control. At the forefront of this movement was Hussein, sherif of Mecca.

As a descendant of the prophet Muhammad and guardian of Islam's holiest places, Hussein enjoyed great prestige within the Arab world. Even before the outbreak of the First World War, Hussein had initiated discussions with Britain for an alliance in the event of hostilities with Turkey. In the course of 1915, Hussein entered into correspondence with the British high commissioner in Egypt, Sir Henry McMahon, which formed the basis for the raising of the Arab revolt against the Turkish Empire in June of the following year. Although Hussein understood Britain to have agreed to Arab independence after the war, a secret accord with the French, known as the Sykes–Picot agreement after the two principal negotiators, laid the foundation for the division of former Turkish territories between Britain and France at the end of the war. Yet more damaging to Arab interests was the declaration in November 1917 by the British foreign secretary, Arthur Balfour, that 'His Majesty's Government view with favour the establishment in Palestine of a national home for the Jewish people'.[1]

From the late nineteenth century, European Jews had been subjected to increasing persecution. Appalled by the intolerance which he saw in his home city of Vienna and elsewhere, the journalist Theodor Herzl penned his 1896 book *Der Judenstaat*, which called for the creation of a Jewish state. The following year, the first Zionist Congress held at Basle in Switzerland proclaimed as its goal the creation of a home for Jews in Palestine. While a number of British statesmen had sympathy with Zionism, the Balfour Declaration can be seen as deriving from expediency rather than genuine commitment to the Zionist cause. By issuing the Declaration, it was hoped that Jews in the United States and Russia would pressure their respective governments to prosecute the war against Germany with more vigour, thus relieving the almost intolerable wartime burdens on Britain. 'The vast majority of Jews in Russia and America', confessed Balfour, 'as indeed, all over the world, now appeared to be favourable to Zionism. If we could make a declaration favourable to such an ideal, we should be able to carry on extremely useful propaganda both in Russia and America.'[2] In the aftermath of war, Britain struggled to honour the conflicting tangle of agreements which she had entered into during the war.

Arab yearning for independence was frustrated by the San Remo Conference of April 1920 at which the League of Nations gave administrative, or mandatory, rights to the French in Syria and Lebanon, and to the British in Iraq and Palestine. Following the Cairo Conference a year later, the eastern part of Palestine was renamed Transjordan and placed under the nominal rulership of Abdullah, one of Hussein's sons. Another son, Feisal, who had been ejected from Syria by the French in July 1920, was installed as king of Iraq. Although Iraq entered the League of Nations in 1932, its independence was limited by the close relationship which it still possessed with Britain. Two years earlier, an Anglo-Iraqi Treaty had established sovereign British rights over the military bases at Habbaniyya and Shaiba near Baghdad and Basra respectively. In addition, Britain reserved the right to use all of Iraq's military facilities in time of war. The relatively successful adjustment of Anglo-Iraqi relations in the inter-war years contrasted with the intractable problems presented by Palestine.

Doubts about the wisdom of holding Palestine were voiced from the outset. Referring in June 1920 to Britain's new responsibilities in the Middle East, the colonial secretary, Winston Churchill, stressed: 'The Palestine venture is the most difficult to withdraw from and the one which certainly will never yield any profit of a material kind.'[3] Riots between Arabs and newly arrived Jewish immigrants in May 1921 confirmed Churchill's fears. In August 1929, disputes over the Western Wall in Jerusalem escalated into widespread violence which left 133 Jews and 116 Arabs dead. Two British commissions set up to look into the disturbances, headed by Sir Walter Shaw and Sir John Hope-Simpson, identified Arab fear of Jewish immigration and land purchase as the root of the problem. The strong Zionist reaction to these reports and the resulting White Paper, forced the weak government of Ramsay MacDonald to reassure the head of the World Zionist Organisation, Chaim Weizmann, that Britain had no intention of limiting Jewish immigration. In consequence, the Jewish population of Palestine grew to 370,483 in a total population of 1,336,518 by 1936. In mollifying the Jews, however, Britain merely succeeded in inflaming the Arabs, who rose in revolt in April 1936. An investigation into the disturbances was carried out by the Palestine Royal Commission under Lord Peel in 1937. The Commission's recommendation that Palestine be partitioned between Jews and Arabs merely intensified the revolt. Britain's apparently pro-Zionist stance, however, began to be revised in the light of wider international considerations.

In October 1935, Italy had invaded Ethiopia, raising the prospect of Italian control of the Red Sea entrance to the Suez Canal in time of war. In such circumstances, reinforcements from India to Egypt would have to be sent overland through Palestine. Palestine's strategic value would be lost, nevertheless, if the country continued in a state of unrest. British statesmen also perceived the need to placate neighbouring Arab states which were beginning to take a keen interest in the plight of their Palestinian brethren. '[W]e are now compelled', admitted the prime minister, Neville Chamberlain, 'to consider the Palestine problem mainly from the point of view of its effects on the international situation . . . if we must offend one side, let us offend the Jews rather than the Arabs.'[4] As a result of such considerations, Britain issued a White Paper in May 1939 which set a limit to Jewish immigration of 75,000 over a five-year period after which further Jewish settlement could only occur with the consent of the Arabs. Britain also offered the in-built Arab majority independence within ten years. The whole basis of the White Paper was undermined as the suffering of European Jewry at the hands of Nazi Germany became known.

At the time of Germany's defeat in May 1945, it is estimated that at least 6 million Jews had been exterminated in Nazi concentrations camps. The scale of Jewish suffering brought the question of the creation of a Jewish homeland in Palestine to the centre of international attention. Partly out of sympathy for the plight of the Jews and partly to secure the Zionist vote in forthcoming elections, the American president, Harry S. Truman, wrote to the British premier Clement

Attlee on 31 August 1945 demanding the immediate admission of 100,000 Jewish refugees into Palestine. In an attempt to involve their American critics in the problems of Palestine, the British established an Anglo-American Commission of Enquiry in November 1945. The Commission's deliberations failed to harmonise British and American policies, prompting Attlee to confide: 'My annoyance is with the Americans who forever lay heavy burdens on us without lifting a little finger to help.'[5] To make matters worse, British personnel became the target for Jewish attacks.

In October 1945, the defence force of the Jewish community in Palestine, the *Haganah*, joined forces with smaller terrorist organisations in armed revolt. By the end of the year, Britain had dispatched 80,000 troops in an attempt to quell the unrest. Jewish forces, nevertheless, scored a number of notable successes, including the blowing up of the British headquarters in the King David Hotel, Jerusalem, on 22 July 1946. Such was the level of disorder in Palestine that its strategic value to Britain was being progressively eroded. What is more, the annual cost of maintaining Britain's military presence had reached the unsustainable figure of £40 million. On 14 February 1947, the British cabinet resolved to refer the whole question to the United Nations.

While the UN deliberated the future of Palestine, Britain struggled to contain the escalation of illegal immigration into the country. With reception camps on the island of Cyprus full, Britain began returning Jewish refugees back to their port of origin amid much international criticism. In a majority report submitted towards the end of August, the United Nations Special Commission on Palestine called for the partition of Palestine and the creation of a separate Jewish state. The British foreign secretary, Ernest Bevin, described the plan as 'manifestly unfair to the Arabs', and persuaded the cabinet on 20 September not only to reject it but also to withdraw from Palestine. The advantages of withdrawal, emphasised Bevin, would be that 'British lives would not be lost, nor British resources expended, in suppressing one Palestinian community to the advantage of the other'.[6] Even the chancellor of the exchequer, Hugh Dalton, who had once been a strong supporter of Zionism, admitted that 'if an agreed settlement could not be reached in Palestine, that country was of no strategic value to HMG and the maintenance of British forces in it merely led to a heavy strain on our financial resources'.[7] Britain's departure from Palestine on 14 May 1948 coincided with the proclamation of the state of Israel. A general Arab–Israeli war followed. In the ensuing chaos, hundreds of thousands of Palestinians were forced to flee their homes, while the armies of the Arab coalition ranged against Israel were defeated. Although Britain's judicious withdrawal had foreclosed the threat of a general Arab campaign against her interests in the Middle East, her role in the creation of Israel left a legacy of bitterness in the Arab world. The persistent crisis in Palestine, moreover, made the settlement of other contentious issues in the region more difficult.

Britain, Egypt and Suez

At the beginning of the First World War, Britain had declared a protectorate over Egypt. The unpopularity of British rule persuaded Britain to make a unilateral declaration of Egyptian independence in 1922. This apparent easing of imperial control was qualified by Britain's retention of control of a number of important areas of government, including the conduct of Egyptian foreign and defence policy. While the 1936 Anglo-Egyptian Treaty formally ended Britain's military occupation of Egypt, British forces were permitted to garrison the Suez Canal zone for a further twenty years.

In 1945, Egypt requested a revision of the 1936 treaty. Subsequent discussions focused on the circumstances in which Britain could use military facilities in Egypt. Bevin and the Egyptian premier, Ismail Sidky, were on the verge of agreement towards the end of 1946 when negotiations foundered on Britain's refusal to countenance an Egyptian reunification with the Sudan. The failure to reach an accord obliged Britain to rely on the discredited 1936 treaty to justify her continued military presence in the Canal zone. Egypt's growing resentment towards Britain was fuelled by the latter's role in the creation of Israel.

Referring to the impact of Egypt's defeat at the hands of Israel in 1948–49, John Darwin has argued that 'Nothing could have been better calculated to . . . redouble Egyptian hostility to Britain on whose "betrayal" of the Palestinian Arabs the catastrophe could conveniently be blamed'.[8] This feeling was given tangible expression in October 1951 when the Egyptian premier, Nahas Pasha, unilaterally abrogated the 1936 treaty. This dramatic gesture failed to save his unpopular government, which soon fell from power. A succession of weak governments followed. Against this unstable background, a group of army officers, led by General Muhammad Neguib and Colonel Gamal Abdel Nasser, staged a successful coup on 23 July 1952. In the power struggle between Neguib and Nasser which followed, the latter emerged triumphant, becoming prime minister in April 1954 and president from June 1956. It was the Suez Crisis which elevated Nasser from leader of Egypt to leader of the Arab world.

Initially Anglo-Egyptian relations experienced a marked improvement. In July 1954 an agreement was reached under which all British forces were to leave Egypt by 18 June 1956. Anglo-Egyptian harmony was short-lived, however. The formation in February 1955 of the Baghdad Pact, a defensive alliance between Iraq and Turkey which Britain subsequently joined, infuriated Nasser, who perceived it as a threat to his regional leadership ambitions. In September, he announced a deal to purchase arms from the Soviet Union, via Czechoslovakia, thus breaking the Western monopoly on the supply of weapons to Egypt. In an attempt to administer a sharp rebuke to the Egyptian president, the United States withdrew its financial support for the construction of the Aswan Dam, a project which Nasser claimed to be vital for the economic development of his country. On 26 July 1956 Nasser's response came with the announcement of the nationalisation of the Suez Canal.

The Canal, which still carried a vast amount of British trade, especially oil, was seen as vital to Britain's prosperity and economic well-being. The British prime minister, Anthony Eden, even described Nasser as having 'his hand on our windpipe'.[9] Eden also told the American president, Dwight D. Eisenhower, that 'The removal of Nasser and the installation in Egypt of a regime less hostile to the West must . . . rank high among our objectives'.[10] Despite Eisenhower's refusal to support the use of force (see document 9.4), Eden moved towards military confrontation with Nasser. During secret discussions between representatives of the British, French, and Israeli governments, at Sèvres, Paris, on 22 October, it was agreed that Israel would attack Egypt, thus providing Britain and France with a justification to dispatch their own troops to Egypt under the guise of separating the combatants and protecting the Canal.

Following the Israeli assault on Egypt on 29 October, Britain and France issued an ultimatum, described by the US secretary of state as 'about as crude and brutal as anything he had ever seen',[11] demanding that Israel and Egypt withdraw 10 miles either side of the Canal to allow an Anglo-French occupation. The Egyptians' rejection of the ultimatum led to the first wave of Anglo-French attacks on 31 October. This action provoked a storm of international criticism, not least from the United States, which not only condemned its allies in the United Nations, but also refused to provide assistance to stabilise Britain's deteriorating financial situation. A week after the attack on Egypt had begun, British forces were ordered to cease fire. On 23 November, Eden flew to Jamaica for rest and convalescence, prompting his former principal private secretary to remark: 'The captain leaves the sinking ship which he has steered personally on to the rocks.'[12] On 9 January 1957, Eden resigned from office, ostensibly on health grounds.

The impact of Suez

The long-term impact of the Suez episode on Britain's international and imperial relations is a complex question. Anglo-American friendship and co-operation were restored following a meeting between Eisenhower and the new British prime minister, Harold Macmillan, at Bermuda in March 1957. Nevertheless, the Suez Crisis underscored the real limits to Britain's freedom of action on the international stage. Britain, as Eden's private secretary, Guy Millard, pointed out, 'could never again resort to military action, outside British territories, without at least American acquiescence'.[13]

On the question of the consequences of Suez on Britain's standing in the Middle East, no simple picture emerges. Certainly Britain's attack on Egypt, in apparent collusion with Israel, shocked the Arab world. In March 1957, the traditionally pro-British regime in Jordan succumbed to pressure to repudiate the 1948 Anglo-Jordanian military alliance. The loyalty of the oil-bearing sheikhdoms of the Persian Gulf was also stretched. Referring specifically to Kuwait, the British representative there, known as the political agent, confessed that 'it is difficult to see how, in the face of an accepted and unquestioned view that we acted in collusion with Israel, we can hope to maintain our previous close relationship of confidence and trust'.[14] The prestige of the monarchical regime in Iraq, upon which Britain had so heavily depended for the maintenance of her regional interests, was severely undermined by Suez. At the beginning of 1957, the British ambassador in Baghdad warned that 'The action of Her Majesty's Government, because it was linked with action by Israel, placed . . . the King and Crown Prince and all those in Iraq who had so actively pursued a policy of friendship with Her Majesty's Government, not only in the gravest political difficulty but in danger of their lives, and imperilled the continued existence of the régime and the monarchy'.[15] This warning proved prophetic. On 14 July 1958, the Iraqi monarchy was swept aside in a bloody revolution.

It would be dangerous, however, to regard Suez as a watershed separating a period of British regional supremacy from one of impotence. On the one hand, Britain, while remaining the dominant power in the Middle East after 1945, had seen her influence progressively eroded. In Saudi Arabia, the United States assumed the political and economic sway once enjoyed by Britain. It can be suggested, moreover, that the nationalisation of the British-owned Anglo-Iranian Oil Company in 1951 by Iranian premier Mohammed Mossadiq was even more damaging to British prestige than Nasser's actions five years later. In the aftermath of Mossadiq's nationalisation of Anglo-Iranian, for instance, the British political agent in Kuwait identified the 'emergence of a belief . . . that it was merely necessary to bark loudly and lengthily enough to make the British let go anywhere'.[16]

On the other hand, while British power had been undermined in the years before 1956, it by no means collapsed after that date. By the summer of 1957, Britain had recovered sufficiently from the Suez reverse to intervene militarily in Oman, where the Sultan of Muscat was facing internal rebellion. In July 1958, furthermore, Britain dispatched troops to Jordan to support the unstable regime of King Hussein. Three years later, British troops arrived in Kuwait to deter an Iraqi attack on the oil-rich sheikhdom. Writing at the end of 1961, the British representative, or political resident, in the Persian Gulf, Sir William Luce, commented that 'Britain at this moment stands more deeply committed in the Persian Gulf, both politically and militarily, than at any time since the last war, a situation which is in marked contrast with the great contraction of our political and military commitments elsewhere in the world over the last fifteen years'.[17] Britain maintained a formal presence in the Persian Gulf until 1971. Four years earlier Britain had departed from Aden in southern Arabia. How would you explain the maintenance of these outposts long after larger Middle Eastern territories had been relinquished?

Document case study

9.1 Shaw Commission on the disturbances in Palestine: report, 12 March 1930

On both sides the political leaders are pursuing different aims with single-minded vigour. Their activities are directed to one aspect of the question only and obstacles which bar the way to the fulfilment of their aims either are totally ignored or are brushed aside as being of no account. The idea of compromise scarcely exists. In the atmosphere which thus prevails all sight is lost of the difficulties of the Administration and every important decision of the Government is hailed by one side or the other as a failure to carry out the principles of the Mandate.

Source: Frederick Madden and John Darwin (eds.), *Dependent empire, 1900–1948: colonies, protectorates, and mandates*, Westport, 1994, pp. 609–10

9.2 Ernest Bevin: HMG's statement of policy on Palestine, 18 February 1947

His Majesty's Government have of themselves no power, under the terms of the Mandate, to award the country either to the Arabs or to the Jews, or even to partition it between them. It is in these circumstances that we have decided that we are unable to accept the scheme put forward either by the Arabs or by the Jews, or to impose ourselves a solution of our own. We have, therefore, reached the conclusion that the only course open to us is to submit the problem to the judgement of the United Nations. We intend to place before them an historical account of the way in which His Majesty's Government have discharged their trust in Palestine over the last 25 years. We shall explain that the Mandate has proved to be unworkable in practice, and that the obligations undertaken to the two communities in Palestine have been shown to be irreconcilable.

Source: Frederick Madden and John Darwin (eds.), *Dependent empire, 1900–1948: colonies, protectorates, and mandates*, Westport, 1994, p. 624

9.3 Letter from Eden to Eisenhower, 6 September 1956

[T]he seizure of the Suez Canal is, we are convinced, the opening gambit in a planned campaign designed by Nasser to expel all Western influence and interests from Arab countries. He believes that if he can get away with this . . . his prestige in Arabia will be so great that he will be able to mount revolutions of young officers in Saudi Arabia, Jordan, Syria and Iraq . . . These new Governments will in effect be Egyptian satellites if not Russian ones. They will have to place their united oil resources under the control of a United Arabia led by Egypt and under Russian influence. When that moment comes Nasser can deny oil to Western Europe and we shall all be at his mercy.

Source: Anthony Gorst and Lewis Johnman, *The Suez Crisis*, London, 1997, pp. 78–79

9.4 Letter from Eisenhower to Eden, 8 September 1956

The use of military force against Egypt under present circumstances might have consequences even more serious than causing the Arabs to support Nasser. It might cause a serious misunderstanding between our two countries because I must say frankly that there is as yet no public opinion in this country which is prepared to support such a move, and the most significant public opinion that there is seems to think that the United Nations was formed to prevent this very thing.

Source: Anthony Gorst and Lewis Johnman, *The Suez Crisis*, London, 1997, pp. 79–80

9.5 Statement by John Foster Dulles (US secretary of state) to the National Security Council, 1 November 1956

For many years now, the US has been walking a tightrope between the effort to maintain our old and valued relations with our British and French allies on the one hand, and on the other try to assure ourselves of the friendship and understanding of the newly independent countries who have escaped from colonialism . . . Unless we now assert and maintain this leadership, all of these newly independent countries will turn from us to the USSR.

Source: Scott Lucas (ed.), *Britain and Suez: the lion's last roar*, Manchester, 1996, p. 98

9.6 Letter from Sir Bernard Burrows (political resident, Persian Gulf) to the Foreign Office, No. 989, 3 November 1956

Apart from the short term danger of strain on loyalty of the responsible element, I am particularly concerned at the long term effect of this situation. Our continued attack on Egypt while doing nothing against Israel is one thing that might make Kuwait and perhaps Qatar think of changing their relationship with us. Since the important object of our Middle East policy is to preserve our position here I submit that full weight should be given to this aspect.

Source: Public Record Office, London, FO 371/120567

9.7 The Suez conspiracy revealed

Shuckburgh was Eden's principal private secretary from 1951 to 1954 and assistant under-secretary at the Foreign Office from 1954 to June 1956.

1 November 1956
Dined with Tony Nutting [minister of state, Foreign Office]. He told me the whole story from the beginning . . . There was the fullest collusion with the Israelis. Selwyn Lloyd [foreign secretary] actually went to Paris incognito to meet Ben-Gurion [Israeli prime minister] with the French. It is true that he did not actually urge Ben-Gurion to make an attack, but he gave him to understand that we would not take a serious view. Later they even knew the date on which it was to take place. They deliberately deceived the Americans and everyone else.

Source: Evelyn Shuckburgh, *Descent to Suez: diaries, 1951–56*, London, 1986, p. 364

9.8 Statement by Eden to the House of Commons, 20 December 1956

I want to say this on the question of foreknowledge and say it quite bluntly to the House, there was not foreknowledge that Israel would attack Egypt – there was not.

Source: Scott Lucas (ed.), *Britain and Suez: the lion's last roar*, Manchester, 1996, p. 112

Document case-study questions

1 Compare the picture of relations between Jews and Arabs presented in 9.1 with that in 9.2.

2 How convincing do you find Eden's interpretation in 9.3 of Nasser's motives in nationalising the Suez Canal?

3 What light do 9.4 and 9.5 shed on the American opposition to the use of force in resolving the Suez Crisis?

4 What does 9.6 tell us about the wider regional implications of Britain's use of force against Egypt in 1956?

5 Evaluate the conflicting evidence in 9.7 and 9.8 about Britain's foreknowledge of the Israeli attack on Egypt.

Notes and references

1 Charles D. Smith, *Palestine and the Arab–Israeli conflict*, 2nd edn, New York, 1992, p. 54.

2 Bernard Porter, *The lion's share: a short history of British imperialism, 1850–1995*, 3rd edn, London, 1996, p. 251.

3 Michael J. Cohen, *Palestine to Israel: from mandate to independence*, London, 1988, p. 2.

4 Cohen, *Palestine to Israel*, p. 121.

5 William Roger Louis, *The British Empire in the Middle East, 1945–1951: Arab nationalism, the United States, and postwar imperialism*, Oxford, 1984, p. 419.

6 Michael J. Cohen, *Palestine and the great powers, 1945–1948*, Princeton, 1982, p. 275.

7 Cohen, *Palestine to Israel*, p. 237.

8 John Darwin, *Britain and decolonisation: the retreat from empire in the post-war world*, Basingstoke, 1988, p. 207.

9 Tony Shaw, *Eden, Suez and the mass media: propaganda and persuasion during the Suez Crisis*, London, 1996, p. 189.

10 Keith Kyle, *Suez*, New York, 1991, p. 179.

11 Geoffrey Warner, 'Review article: the United States and the Suez Crisis', *International Affairs*, vol. 67 (1991): 314.

12 Evelyn Shuckburgh, *Descent to Suez: diaries, 1951–56*, London, 1986, p. 365.

13 Anthony Adamthwaite, 'Suez revisited', *International Affairs*, vol. 64 (1988): 449.

14 Letter from G. W. Bell to Sir Bernard Burrows, 9 November 1956, Public Record Office, London, FO 371/120557.

15 William Roger Louis, 'The British and the origins of the Iraqi Revolution', in Robert A. Fernea and William Roger Louis (eds.), *The Iraqi Revolution of 1958: the old social classes revisited*, London, 1991, p. 43.

16 Kuwait Administrative Report for 1951, Public Record Office, London, FO 371/98323.

17 Letter from Sir William Luce to the Earl of Home, no. 98, 22 November 1961, Public Record Office, London, FO 371/156670.

10 End of empire: Africa

Key dates

1938 Publication of Lord Hailey's *African survey*
1940 Colonial Development and Welfare Act
1941 Atlantic Charter
1942 Fall of Singapore
1945 Colonial Development and Welfare Act
1947 Local Government Despatch
1948 Accra Riots
1953 Creation of the Central African Federation
1957 The Gold Coast (Ghana) becomes independent
1959 Declaration of a state of emergency in Nyasaland
      Iain Macleod becomes colonial secretary
1960 Nigeria becomes independent
1963 Kenya becomes independent
1964 Nyasaland (Malawi) and Northern Rhodesia (Zambia) become independent

While the empires of her European rivals collapsed as a result of the First World War, Britain's emerged from the conflict apparently unscathed, even enhanced. Soon after armistice, the commander-in-chief in India remarked proudly: 'Now that it is all over and the Empire stands on a pinnacle built by her tenacity and courage – never did our reputation stand as high.'[1] Such optimism proved ill-founded, however. In the inter-war years the empire was squeezed between the vice of domestic restrictions and foreign pressures: newly enfranchised voters demanded greater expenditure on social provisions, while international rivals posed new threats to Britain's far-flung imperial possessions. The Second World War witnessed a temporary revival in the empire, as imperial resources were systematically mobilised in pursuit of final victory. Britain also sought to refurbish her imperial image through the promotion of economic and political reform. In the post-war years, nevertheless, further international and domestic pressures, coupled with the growth of colonial nationalism, sounded the death-knell of the empire.

From trusteeship to partnership

After 1918, Britain found herself in the invidious position of needing imperial resources as never before to bolster her foundering economy, while lacking the means by which to cover her increased colonial commitments. One of the principal devices employed by Britain to overcome this dilemma was to develop and extend collaborative relationships with elites within the empire. In Africa this expedient was raised to the status of a declared policy which became known as indirect rule.

Developed by Lord Lugard in Nigeria and given detailed articulation in his *Dual mandate in Tropical Africa*, first published in 1922, indirect rule involved ruling through local potentates, typically chiefs, kings or emirs, whose powers were recognised and developed as instruments of local administration. The system's principal advantage was its relative cheapness, a particularly important consideration in the context of the straitened economic circumstances in which Britain found herself after 1918. By delegating local functions such as policing and revenue collection to traditional rulers, Britain's administrative costs were kept to a minimum. The policy could also be justified on the grounds that Britain was fulfilling the role of trustee for her African territories: by preserving the position of the chiefs, it was claimed, indigenous society was being protected. In the late 1930s, however, indirect rule began to be questioned. This can be accounted for in a number of ways.

Widespread riots in the West Indies in 1937 and 1938, although not directly connected with Africa, jolted the Colonial Office out of its complacency by highlighting that not all was well within the colonial empire. This process continued with the publication in 1938 of Lord Hailey's *African survey*. Hailey, a former member of the Indian civil service who retrained to become an expert on African affairs, emphasised the urgent need for social and economic development in Britain's African territories, as well as the problems of integrating indirect rule with parliamentary institutions. With the appointment of Malcolm MacDonald as colonial secretary, also in 1938, Hailey's ideas found a receptive pupil.

'Even amongst the most backward races of Africa', pledged MacDonald in June, 'our main effort is to teach those peoples to stand always a little more securely on their own feet.'[2] MacDonald was also instrumental in steering the Colonial Development and Welfare Act through parliament in 1940, which promised to provide £55 million for the colonies over ten years. By providing substantial sums for colonial development from the British exchequer, Britain was not only breaking the tradition that the colonies should be financially self-sufficient, but also demonstrating to the world her generosity and, as MacDonald put it, 'faith in ultimate victory'.[3] Indeed, the presentation of British colonial policy assumed new importance in the context of Britain's global struggle against the axis powers. 'We cannot afford', stressed the Ministry of Information, 'to ride rough-shod over the peoples of the Colonies whilst maintaining to the World at large we are fighting for the freedom of mankind.'[4] The need to refashion Britain's imperial image assumed yet more urgency following the loss of Singapore.

Singapore, reputed to be an impregnable base, fell to the invading Japanese in February 1942 exposing the whole British imperial position in Asia and the Pacific to attack. To make matters worse, the colonial peoples of Southeast Asia demonstrated a marked disinclination to come to Britain's aid. In seeking to deflect criticism, both domestic and international, Britain began to speak the language of reform, the old concept of trusteeship being replaced with that of partnership (see document 10.2). In July 1943, moreover, the colonial secretary, Oliver Stanley, pledged Britain to 'guide Colonial people along the road to self-government within the framework of the British Empire'.[5] Such statements were valuable in countering American pressure on the British imperial position.

In August 1941, the US president, Franklin D. Roosevelt, and the British prime minister, Winston Churchill, issued the Atlantic Charter in which they expressed their joint wish to see 'sovereign rights and self-government restored to those who have been forcibly deprived of them'. Although Churchill later restricted the commitment to 'the restoration of the sovereignty, self-government and national life of the States and nations of Europe now under the Nazi yoke', the Atlantic Charter symbolised American scepticism towards European empires. *Life* magazine, reflecting the views of the American people, declared in October 1942: 'one thing we are sure we are not fighting for is to hold the British Empire together'.[6] Under the pressure of such opinions, the British began to plan a new, more ambitious, development programme for the colonies. 'As regards money', noted a Treasury official, 'we are conscious that we must justify ourselves before the world as a great Colonial Power.'[7] In March 1945, Britain unveiled a new Colonial Development and Welfare Act which made £120 million available to the colonies over a period of ten years. Money unspent from one year's allocation, furthermore, could be carried over to the next. Britain's new-found commitment to the colonies continued into the post-war years. Britain's interests, however, were not completely altruistic.

During the Second World War, British Africa's economic potential was systematically exploited for the first time. 'Now that we have lost Malaya', asserted the colonial secretary, Lord Cranborne, in March 1942, 'the main problem before our African Administrators . . . is to make good as far as the resources of their Territories allow the commodities formerly drawn from the Far East.'[8] In the aftermath of war the economic resources of Africa were no less important.

The long years of war had a devastating effect on the British economy. It is estimated that 25 per cent of Britain's national wealth was lost between 1939 and 1945. Foreign assets, especially dollar investments, had been liquidated to pay for vital imports, while British exports through the war years fell to 40 per cent of their pre-war levels. As the Colonial Office was forced to concede: 'In effect, the United Kingdom has fought this war with complete disregard for financial consequences, and has poured into it the accumulated capital of generations of saving.'[9] Just before the defeat of Japan, the economist J. M. Keynes warned that Britain was facing a 'financial Dunkirk'. In these circumstances, the commodity-producing territories of Africa and Southeast Asia were prized for their exports to the United States, where they earned valuable dollars for the sterling area.

If Britain 'pushed on and developed Africa', predicted the foreign secretary, Ernest Bevin, 'we could have the United States dependent on us and eating out of our hands in five years'.[10] The colonies were also central to Bevin's vision of Britain as an independent 'Third Force' in the world. 'We have the material resources in the Colonial Empire, if we develop them', he argued, 'and by giving a spiritual lead now we should be able to carry out our main task in a way which will show clearly that we are not subservient to the United States of America or the Soviet Union.'[11] In pursuit of such policy objectives, an army of experts were sent to Africa from Britain in what has become known as the 'second colonial occupation'. It was increasingly recognised, however, that successful economic development was also dependent on the co-operation of educated Africans.

As early as 1943, the director of recruitment to the colonial service had prophesied that 'the educated native is bound to become to a great extent the future mouthpiece and leader of his people . . . the new policy of partnership cannot work without him'.[12] After the war, it was the responsibility of the colonial secretary, Arthur Creech Jones, and the head of the Africa division at the Colonial Office, Andrew Cohen, to put such ideals into practice.

In his Local Government Despatch to African governors of 25 February 1947, Creech Jones wrote: 'I believe that the key to success lies in the development of an efficient and democratic system of local government.'[13] In May, a committee of Colonial Office officials charged with charting a 'new approach' to Africa came to the conclusion that 'within a generation . . . the principal African territories will have attained . . . full responsible government'.[14] Colonial Office confidence, nevertheless, was shaken by disturbances in Accra, the capital of the Gold Coast, at the end of February 1948. The Watson Committee, established to investigate the causes of the troubles, concluded that 'in the conditions existing today in the Gold Coast a substantial measure of reform is necessary to meet the legitimate aspirations of the indigenous population'. The specific details of constitutional change were considered by an all-African 38-member committee under Mr Justice Henry Coussey. Reporting in August 1949, the committee advocated an assembly of nationally elected representatives, eight of whom would become ministers on the Governor's Executive Council. Largely accepted by the British government, the Coussey Committee's proposals represented a major step forward in the Gold Coast's movement towards self-government. The Gold Coast's emerging nationalist leaders, however, were far from satisfied.

The winds of change

In 1921, the colonial secretary, Winston Churchill, had described the African colonies as possessing a 'docile, tractable population'.[15] By the late 1940s, the same could not be said with any accuracy. The experience of the Second World War, during which many Africans were recruited to fight overseas while more still were forcibly employed as labourers in schemes connected with the war, had a profound impact. On the one hand, expectations had been raised by wartime promises and by the fact that returning African soldiers had become accustomed

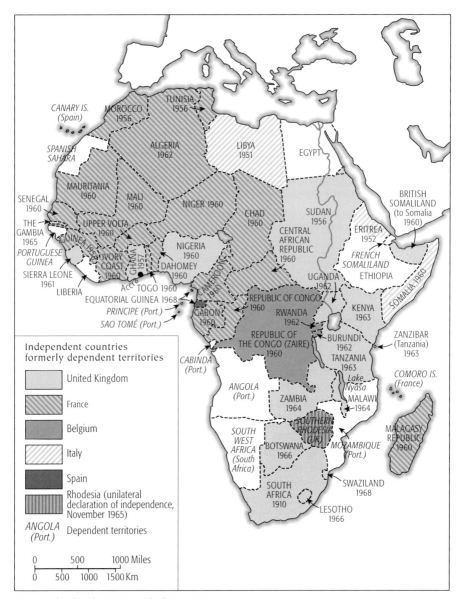

Map 8. The decolonisation of Africa, 1956–68

to the welfare system of the armed forces. On the other, rising costs of living and mounting unemployment in the aftermath of war fuelled discontent with the colonial state. Such discontent could be exploited by nationalist politicians, one of the most influential of whom was Kwame Nkrumah of the Gold Coast.

In 1949, Nkrumah had formed the Convention People's Party (CPP), which at the beginning of the following year launched a campaign of 'positive action' for 'self-government now'. Despite Nkrumah's swift arrest, his party triumphed at elections held in 1951, whereupon the recently appointed governor, Charles Arden-Clarke, summoned him from gaol to become leader of government business. Following CPP victories at two further elections, in 1954 and 1956, the Gold Coast became the independent state of Ghana on 6 March 1957 (see Map 8). Britain's other principal West Africa territory, Nigeria, followed Ghana into independence in 1960. Progress towards independence in Britain's East and Central African territories was less smooth, however.

The existence of white settler communities in Kenya, Southern and Northern Rhodesia, and Nyasaland was a complicating factor in the decolonisation process which defied easy solutions. Kenya's problems were compounded by the outbreak of an anti-colonial rising in 1952, known as the Mau Mau Rebellion, which was not finally extinguished until 1960. As late as 1959, the colonial secretary, Alan Lennox-Boyd, predicted that Kenya would not achieve independence until 1975.

In central Africa, in 1953, Britain sponsored an ill-fated federation of the two Rhodesias and Nyasaland largely in an attempt to prevent Southern Rhodesia, with its large white minority, from gravitating towards white-dominated South Africa. The multi-racialism which underpinned the British calculations for the Central African Federation failed to materialise and the resulting white domination alienated the black majority. In July 1958, Dr Hastings Banda returned to his native Nyasaland from London to lead the country's opposition to the Federation. In Northern Rhodesia, Kenneth Kaunda became the leading African spokesman against the Federation.

Matters came to a head in March 1959 when a state of emergency was declared in Nyasaland following rumours that Banda and his followers were planning to murder prominent whites. The declaration of emergency, however, merely seemed to provoke violence and on 3 March 20 Africans were shot dead in disturbances at Nkata Bay on Lake Nyasa. A commission of inquiry into the whole affair conducted by a judge, Sir Patrick Devlin, concluded that not only was the evidence for a 'murder-plot' insufficient to justify the action taken, but also that Nyasaland had descended to the position of a 'police state'. This harsh judgement followed hard on the heels of the shocking revelation that 11 Mau Mau detainees had been beaten to death in Hola camp in Kenya. It was against the background of these inauspicious circumstances that Iain Macleod became colonial secretary in October 1959.

Despite holding this office for only two years, the pace of decolonisation accelerated rapidly under Macleod's stewardship. His approach to colonial affairs was one which accepted that Britain could not contain and control African nationalism and that a 'deliberate speeding up of the movement towards independence' was necessary in order to prevent bloodshed in Africa (see document 10.6). Macleod also accepted the view that political developments in West Africa were bound to have an impact elsewhere on the continent. '[I]ndependence once given to the African in the Gold Coast', he wrote, 'could not long be denied to his brother in Kenya.'[16] Perhaps most importantly, Macleod appears to have been motivated by genuine egalitarianism, which was an essential precondition for the acceptance of black majority rule in those territories with a white settler minority.

One of Macleod's most significant decisions was to release Hastings Banda from prison and invite him to London. The resulting talks paved the way for a general election in Nyasaland in August 1961 which Banda's Malawi Congress Party overwhelmingly won. At the end of 1962, Britain recognised Nyasaland's right to secede from the Federation. By July 1964, Nyasaland, renamed Malawi, had achieved independence. At the time of the Northern Rhodesian constitutional conference in January 1961, Macleod identified Kenneth Kaunda's United National Independence Party as representing the best chance of future peace and progress. His commitment to recognising the primacy of black African voters was reflected in his February 1961 White Paper on Northern Rhodesia. Macleod's work was continued by his successor, Reginald Maudling, who a year later announced changes in the North Rhodesian constitution which opened the possibility of African majority rule. General elections in 1962 and 1964 paved the way for Northern Rhodesia's secession from the Federation and subsequent independence as the new state of Zambia in October 1964. Macleod's influence can also be detected in the progress of Kenya to independent status.

At the Lancaster House Conference in January 1960, African delegates demanded Kenya's early independence and the release of Jomo Kenyatta, the man who Britain had held responsible for the Mau Mau Rebellion. Although Macleod resisted the second demand, he announced changes in the Kenyan constitution which opened the prospect of African majority rule in place of the white-dominated multi-racialism. In August 1961, Kenyatta was finally released, leading his country to independence in December 1963.

Macleod was assisted in his endeavour to accelerate the pace of decolonisation and introduce black majority rule by the full support which he received from the prime minister, Harold Macmillan. Macmillan in turn was able to back his colonial secretary's radical policies, despite unease within the Conservative Party, on account of his large majority in the House of Commons following the 1959 general election. Macmillan was also influenced by the speed with which France and Belgium brought their colonial empires in Africa to an end. In 1960, 16 new African nations entered the United Nations, most of which were no more politically mature, and some less so, than the British colonies. In order to maintain her image as a responsible and responsive decoloniser, therefore, Britain felt obliged to speed up the pace of change in her African possessions (see document 10.4). In sponsoring rapid withdrawal from empire, moreover, the Macmillan government was looking to maintain her economic and political interests in the post-independence era by transferring power to moderate nationalists who would continue to be well-disposed towards Britain. Some have even suggested that the decolonisation process represents an attempt by Britain to return to 'informal empire'.[17]

At the time of Macmillan's resignation towards the end of 1963, most of the territories of the British Empire had either achieved independence or were close to achieving it. Although the Labour prime minister, Harold Wilson, still felt able to assert his confidence in Britain's world role, by the late 1960s all that remained of the British Empire were problem territories such as Southern Rhodesia, whose white minority had made a unilateral declaration of independence in 1965, and Ulster, which descended into communal violence in 1968–69, requiring the stationing of British troops in the province. With the handing back to China of Hong Kong in 1997, the last major retreat from empire has been played out.

Document case study

10.1 Minute by G. F. Seel (assistant secretary, Colonial Office) on the integration of indirect rule into a parliamentary system of government, 11 April 1939

We ought to be on our guard against overdoing academic discussion, and ascribing to the theory of indirect rule a divinity of inspiration which it does not really possess . . . If we are frank, we shall admit that where we have employed this system we have done so because, for financial or other reasons, no other means lay ready to our hands of spreading orderly government and the rudiments of social services . . . I feel . . . that in any discussions about indirect rule we should be careful not to regard it as necessarily superior to other systems or destined to survive beyond the initial stages of political development. As regards the immediate action to be taken, while the publication of the 'African Survey' does not in itself mark any turning point in history, I agree that its careful study of the existing position cannot be left unnoticed by the Colonial Office.

Source: S. R. Ashton and S. E. Stockwell (eds.), *Imperial policy and colonial practice, 1925–1945*, part 1, London, 1996, pp. 292, 293

10.2 Speech by Lord Hailey in the House of Lords, 20 May 1942

The use of the term [trusteeship] is irritating to Colonial people. It was intensely unpopular in India. It is becoming equally unpopular in the Colonies, for it has implications on which it is unnecessary to enlarge but which, if I were a native of the Colonies, I should equally resent. If we need to express ourselves in a formula at all, let our relations be those of senior and junior partners in the same enterprise, and let it be said that our contract of partnership involves the progressive increase of the share which the junior partners have in the conduct of the undertaking.

Source: Frederick Madden and John Darwin (eds.), *The dependent empire, 1900–1948: colonies, protectorates, and mandates*, Westport, 1994, p. 35

10.3 'Future provision for colonial development and welfare', memorandum by Oliver Stanley (secretary of state for colonies), 15 November 1944

I am not pretending that the assistance to the Colonies which I propose will not impose some burden upon this country. I do, however, feel that the Colonial Empire means so much to us that we should be prepared to assume some burden for its future. If we are unable or unwilling to do so, are we justified in retaining, or shall we be able to retain, a Colonial Empire? The burden, however, is infinitesimal compared to the gigantic sums in which we are and shall be dealing. Nor is the apparent burden wholly real. If these sums are wisely spent, and the plans devoted to increasing the real productive power of the Colonies, there will in the long run accrue considerable benefit to us, either in the form of increased exports to us of commodities which otherwise we should have to obtain from hard currency countries, or in the form of increased exports from the Colonies as part of the sterling area to the hard currency countries outside.

Source: S. R. Ashton and S. E. Stockwell (eds.), *Imperial policy and colonial practice, 1925–1945*, part 2, London, 1996, p. 205

10.4 'Africa: the next ten years', paper by the Cabinet Official Committee on Africa, 3 June 1959

It must not be forgotten that, after Nigeria becomes independent in 1960, the period of British leadership of the advance of African colonial territories towards independence will appear to be over; and unless we can solve the problems of East and Central Africa, our past record of benevolent government will be forgotten and it will be the French and perhaps the Belgians who will be regarded by world opinion as the leaders, while we may be classed with the Portuguese as obstacles to further advance. Moreover, although conditions have hitherto enabled us to adopt an apparently more simple and unambiguous approach to the problems of black West Africa than to those of the multi-racial societies in East and Central Africa, the growth of Pan-Africanism on a continental scale will make it increasingly difficult for us to continue to pursue policies which, to the African mind, seem to differentiate between the two areas.

Source: AF (59) 28, Public Record Office, London, CAB 134/1355

10.5 Speech by Harold Macmillan to both Houses of the parliament of the Union of South Africa, Cape Town, 3 February 1960

We have seen the awakening of national consciousness in peoples who have for centuries lived in dependence upon some other power. Fifteen years ago this movement spread through Asia. Many countries there of different races and civilisations pressed their claim to an independent national life. Today the same thing is happening in Africa and the most striking of all the impressions I have formed since I left London a month ago is of the strength of this African national consciousness. In different places it takes different forms but it is happening everywhere. The wind of change is blowing through this continent and, whether we like it or not, this growth of national consciousness is a political fact. We must all accept it as a fact, and our national policies must take account of it.

Source: A. N. Porter and A. J. Stockwell (eds.), *British imperial policy and decolonization, 1938–1964*, 2 vols., Basingstoke, 1987–89, vol. 2, pp. 524–25

10.6 'Trouble in Africa', leading article by Iain Macleod in *The Spectator*, 31 January 1964

It has been said that after I became Colonial Secretary there was a deliberate speeding-up of the movement towards independence. I agree. There was. And in my view any other policy would have led to terrible bloodshed in Africa. This is the heart of the argument . . . Were the countries ready for Independence? Of course not . . . The march of men towards their freedom can be guided but not halted. Of course there were risks in moving quickly. But the risks of moving slowly were far greater.

Source: A. N. Porter and A. J. Stockwell (eds.), *British imperial policy and decolonization, 1938–1964*, 2 vols., Basingstoke, 1987–89, vol. 2, pp. 570, 571

Document case-study questions

1 Comment on the assessment of indirect rule in 10.1.

2 In what ways do 10.2 and 10.3 reflect changing British attitudes towards empire?

3 What insights does 10.4 give into the development of British thinking towards Africa?

4 Compare the arguments in favour of rapid decolonisation in 10.5 with those in 10.6.

5 Assess the strengths and weaknesses of 10.6 as a historical source.

Notes and references

1 A. J. Stockwell, 'The war and the British empire', in John Turner (ed.), *Britain and the First World War*, London, 1988, p. 42.

2 John Flint, 'Planned decolonization and its failure in British Africa', *African Affairs*, vol. 82 (1983): 398.

3 S. R. Ashton and S. E. Stockwell (eds.), *Imperial policy and colonial practice, 1925–1945*, part 1, London, 1996, p. lxix.

4 Rosaleen Smyth, 'Britain's African colonies and British propaganda during the Second World War', *Journal of Imperial and Commonwealth History*, vol. 14 (1985): 76.

5 Ashton and Stockwell, *Imperial policy and colonial practice*, part 1, p. 197 n. 4.

6 William Roger Louis and Ronald Robinson, 'The United States and the liquidation of British Empire in Tropical Africa, 1941–1951', in Prosser Gifford and William Roger Louis (eds.), *The transfer of power in Africa: decolonization, 1940–1960*, New Haven, 1982, p. 33.

7 Louis and Robinson, 'Liquidation of British Empire in Tropical Africa', pp. 38–39.

8 Michael Cowen and Nicholas Westcott, 'British imperial economic policy during the war', in David Killingray and Richard Rathbone (eds.), *Africa and the Second World War*, London, 1986, p. 44.

9 'Financial results of the war in the United Kingdom': Colonial Office memorandum, 27 September 1945, CO 852/555/4, cited in Ronald Hyam (ed.), *The Labour government and the end of empire*, part 2, London, 1992, p. 8.

10 Robert Holland, *The pursuit of greatness: Britain and the world role, 1900–1970*, London, 1991, p. 225.

11 John D. Hargreaves, *Decolonization in Africa*, 2nd edn, London, 1996, p. 113.

12 Ashton and Stockwell, *Imperial policy and colonial practice*, part 1, p. 34.

13 R. D. Pearce, *The turning point in Africa: British colonial policy, 1938–48*, London, 1982, p. 148.

14 Louis and Robinson, 'Liquidation of British Empire in Tropical Africa', p. 42.

15 Bernard Porter, *The lion's share: a short history of British imperialism, 1850–1995*, 3rd edn, London, 1996, p. 294.

16 David Goldsworthy, *Colonial issues in British politics, 1945–1961*, Oxford, 1971, p. 364.

17 William Roger Louis and Ronald Robinson, 'The imperialism of decolonization', *Journal of Imperial and Commonwealth History*, vol. 22 (1994): 462–511.

Conclusion

The 'public mind in India', declared T. B. Macaulay in 1833,

> having become instructed in European knowledge, . . . may, in some future age, demand European institutions. Whether such a day will ever come I know not. But never will I attempt to avert or retard it. Whenever it comes, it will be the proudest day in English history.[1]

Despite such pious sentiments, Britain's approach to empire was firmly rooted in a clear conception of her own national interest. Although the rhetoric of empire changed in the two centuries and more surveyed in this book, the underlying pragmatism rarely wavered. Britain pursued her imperial path not out of a sense of altruism, or even primarily concern for indigenous peoples, but for profit, whether in economic, political or military terms. When the balance of advantage shifted, and the burdens of empire outweighed the assets, Britain withdrew. The transfer of power to a partitioned India in 1947 is perhaps the best example of this. Despite the concern of British ministers that a precipitate withdrawal from the subcontinent without securing the rights of Indian minorities would be an 'inglorious end to our long association with India',[2] Britain's post-war impoverishment, coupled with India's declining imperial value, dictated a hasty departure. Nevertheless, profitable territories, such the dollar-earning dependencies of Africa and Southeast Asia, were retained and developed in an effort to stimulate domestic economic recovery in the aftermath of the Second World War. As with India 10 years earlier, by 1957 the value of Britain's remaining dependencies also began to be questioned. Within days of becoming prime minister, Harold Macmillan was requesting 'something like a profit and loss account for each of our Colonial possessions, so that we may be better able to gauge whether, from the financial and economic point of view, we are likely to gain or lose by its departure'.[3] By the 1960s all pretence of preparing territories for independence was abandoned as Britain dispensed with her remaining possessions with alarming speed. As the Foreign Office confessed in 1965 following the decision to leave Aden by 1968 at the latest: 'we have only three years to complete our task. As for about 120 years we barely started it, it is too late to be perfectionist.'[4]

Notes and references

1 Bernard Porter, *The lion's share: a short history of British imperialism, 1850–1995*, 3rd edn, London, 1996, p. 21.

2 'India: constitutional position': cabinet conclusions, 10 December 1946, CAB 128/8, cited in Ronald Hyam (ed.), *The Labour government and the end of empire, 1945–1951*, part 1, London, 1992, p. 32.

3 Cited in A. N. Porter and A. J. Stockwell (eds.), *British imperial policy and decolonization, 1938–64*, vol. 2, Basingstoke, 1989, p. 451.

4 'Defence review: withdrawal from the Aden Base', note by the Foreign Office, 20 December 1965, OPD (O) (AS) (65) 6, Public Record Office, London, CAB 148/49.

Select bibliography

Printed primary sources

Seven volumes of *Select documents on the constitutional history of the British Empire*, Westport and New York, 1985–94, the first five of which have been edited by Frederick Madden and David Fieldhouse, the six and seventh by Madden and John Darwin, provide invaluable documentary sources for the study of the British Empire from early times through to 1948.

Twelve volumes edited by Nicholas Mansergh on *Constitutional relations between Britain and India: the transfer of power, 1942–47*, London, 1970–83, are essential for the study of the end of the British raj in India.

The *British documents on end of empire project* is in the process of producing a definitive collection of documents. The first part of each of the following contains a searching examination of its subject: S. R. Ashton and S. E. Stockwell (eds.), *Imperial policy and colonial practice, 1925–1945*, 2 parts, London, 1996; Ronald Hyam (ed.), *The Labour government and the end of empire, 1945–1951*, 4 parts, London, 1992; David Goldsworthy (ed.), *The Conservative government and the end of empire, 1951–7*, 3 parts, London, 1994; Richard Rathbone (ed.), *Ghana*, 2 parts, London, 1993; A. J. Stockwell (ed.), *Malaya*, 3 parts, London, 1995; K. M. de Silva (ed.), Sri Lanka, 2 parts, London, 1997.

Secondary sources
General and introductory

C. A. Bayly's *Imperial meridian: the British Empire and the world, 1780–1830*, London, 1989 and Bernard Porter's *The lion's share: a short history of British imperialism, 1850–1995*, 3rd edn, London, 1996, serve not merely as introductions to imperial history, but also as perceptive works of historical scholarship. The best single volume dealing with the whole period covered by this book is D. K. Fieldhouse's *The Colonial empires: a comparative survey from the eighteenth century*, 2nd edn, 1982. Containing fascinating illustrations, as well as a stimulating text by a number of leading imperial historians, P. J. Marshall's edited *Cambridge illustrated history of the British Empire*, Cambridge, 1996, serves as an accessible introduction to the subject. Narrative accounts are provided by T. O. Lloyd, *The British Empire, 1558–1983*, Oxford, 1984; Lawrence James, *The rise and fall of the British Empire*, London, 1994; and Martin Kitchen, *The British Empire and Commonwealth: a short history*, Basingstoke, 1996. A more idiosyncratic treatment is offered by Denis Judd's *Empire: the British imperial experience from 1765 to the present*, London, 1996. Maps are essential for the study of empire and these are provided in A. N. Porter's edited work, *Atlas of British overseas expansion*, London, 1991.

Studies of Britain's place in the world since the late eighteenth century include: Muriel E. Chamberlain, *'Pax Britannica'?: British foreign policy, 1789–1914*, London, 1988; David Reynolds, *Britannia overruled: British policy and world power in the 20th century*, London, 1991.

Substantial pioneering studies on the end of empire include R. F. Holland's *European decolonization, 1918–1981: an introductory survey*, Basingstoke, 1985, and John Darwin's *Britain and decolonization: the retreat from empire in the post-war world*, Basingstoke, 1988. A. N. Porter and A. J. Stockwell's, *British imperial policy and decolonization, 1938–1964*, 2 vols., Basingstoke, 1987 and 1989, contains useful introductions to documents focusing on policy-making in London.

1 The Seven Years War and crisis in North America

While written over thirty years ago, I. R. Christie's *Crisis of empire: Great Britain and the American colonies, 1754–1783*, London, 1966, still represents the most valuable introduction to the loss of the American colonies. Containing a very readable text, as well as some well-chosen documents, Peter D. G. Thomas' *Revolution in America: Britain and the colonies, 1763–1776*, Cardiff, 1992, is also worth referring to. A review of the historiography is provided by I. R. Christie's chapter 'The historians' quest for the American Revolution', in Anne Whiteman, J. S. Bromley and P. G. M. Dickson (eds.), *Statesmen, scholars, and merchants*, Oxford, 1973. The impact of the Seven Years War on North America is dealt with in Jack P. Greene's 'The Seven Years' War and the American Revolution: the causal relationship reconsidered', *Journal of Imperial and Commonwealth History*, vol. 8 (1980). For a survey of British attitudes to empire in this period, see P. J. Marshall, 'Empire and authority in the later eighteenth century', *Journal of Imperial and Commonwealth History*, vol. 15 (1987). Bernard Bailyn's ground-breaking *The ideological origins of the American Revolution*, Cambridge, Mass., 1967, is also essential reading.

2 Establishment of Empire in Asia and the Pacific

P. J. Marshall's *Bengal: the British bridgehead: eastern India, 1740–1828*, Cambridge, 1987, and C. A. Bayly's *Indian society and the making of the British Empire*, Cambridge, 1988, are vivid introductions to the growth of empire in India. The military dimension to British expansion in India is examined in Marshall's 'British expansion in India in the eighteenth century: a historical revision', *History*, vol. 60 (1975); his 'Economic and political expansion: the case of Oudh', *Modern Asian Studies*, vol. 9 (1975), provides a specific case study of the process of British expansion. Philip Lawson's *The East India Company: a history*, London, 1993, provides a very readable account of that organisation's contribution to the growth of British power in India.

For interpretations favouring an imperial explanation for the British decision to colonise New South Wales, see Geoffrey Blainey, *The tyranny of distance: how distance shaped Australia's history*, Melbourne, 1968, and Alan Frost's two books, *Convicts and empire: a naval question, 1776–1811*, Melbourne, 1980, and *Botany Bay mirages: illusions of Australia's convict beginnings*, Melbourne, 1994. On the other side of the debate, see Mollie Gillen, 'The Botany Bay decision: convicts not empire', *English Historical Review*, vol. 97 (1982), and D. L. Mackay's two articles, 'Direction and purpose in British imperial policy, 1783–1801', *Historical Journal*, vol. 17 (1974), and 'Far-flung empire: a neglected imperial outpost at Botany Bay, 1788–1801', *Journal of Imperial and Commonwealth History*, vol. 9 (1981).

3 Self-determination in the colonies of European settlement

The starting point for any examination of the colonies of European settlement and the development of the Commonwealth is Nicholas Mansergh's two-volume *The Commonwealth experience*, London, 1982 (first published in 1969 as a single volume). A reassessment of the Durham Report is offered in Ged Martin's 'The influence of the Durham Report', in Ronald Hyam and Ged Martin (eds.), *Reappraisals in British imperial history*, London, 1975. British attitudes towards closer association of the territories of British North America are traced in Martin's *The causes of Canadian confederation, 1837–1867*, Basingstoke, 1995. J. M. Ward's *Colonial self-government: the British experience*, London, 1976, is essential reading for the growth of responsible government in the nineteenth century.

The role of the empire, including the self-governing dominions, in the First World War is examined in the following chapters: A. J. Stockwell, 'The war and the British Empire', in John Turner (ed.), *Britain and the First World War*, London, 1988, and Stephan Constantine, 'Britain and the empire', in Stephan Constantine, Maurice H. Kirby and Mary B. Rose (eds.), *The First World War and Britain*, London, 1995.

For accounts of the development of Anglo-dominion relations in the inter-war years, see R. F. Holland, *Britain and the Commonwealth alliance, 1918–39*, London, 1981, and John Darwin, 'Imperialism in decline? Tendencies in British imperial policy between the wars', *Historical Journal*, vol. 23 (1980).

4 Humanitarianism, anti-slavery and missionary activity

An accessible introduction to slavery within the British Empire is provided by James Walvin's *Slavery and slaves: the British colonial experience*, Manchester, 1992. Eric Williams' controversial and enduring *Capitalism and slavery*, London, 1964 (first published 1944) is essential reading for the economic interpretation of the demise of slavery and the slave trade. Williams' most trenchant critic is Seymour Drescher, who in his *Econocide: British slavery in the era of abolition*, Pittsburgh, 1977, gives a detailed rebuttal of the Williams thesis. Barbara L. Solow and Stanley L. Engerman's edited work, *British capitalism and Caribbean slavery: the legacy of Eric Williams*, Cambridge, 1987, contains a useful set of essays by leading scholars. An analysis of the parliamentary manoeuvrings surrounding the abolition of the slave trade is supplied by Roger Anstey's *The Atlantic slave trade and British abolition, 1760–1810*, New Jersey, 1975. The impact of slavery on Britain is dealt with in Walvin's edited work, *Slavery and British society, 1776–1846*. For the role of women in the anti-slavery campaigns, see Clare Midgely, *Women against slavery: the British campaigns, 1780–1870*, London, 1992.

The best general study of missionaries and empire is provided by Brian Stanley's, *The Bible and the flag: Protestant missions and British imperialism in the nineteenth and twentieth centuries*, Leicester, 1990. A. N. Porter's 'Religion and empire: British expansion in the long nineteenth century', *Journal of Imperial and Commonwealth History*, vol. 20 (1992), is also a stimulating survey. Anthony J. Dachs', 'Missionary imperialism – the case of Bechuanaland', *Journal of African History*, vol. 13 (1972), examines a specific example of missionary influence on British expansion. Contrasting interpretations of the link between Christianity and commerce are offered in Stanley's '"Commerce and Christianity": providence theory, the missionary movement and the imperialism of free trade, 1842–1860', *Historical Journal*, vol. 26 (1983) and Porter's '"Commerce and Christianity": the rise and fall of a nineteenth-century missionary slogan', *Historical Journal*, vol. 28 (1985). The impact of missions on indigenous societies is examined in Porter's recent article, '"Cultural imperialism" and Protestant missionary enterprise, 1780–1914', *Journal of Imperial and Commonwealth History*, vol. 25 (1997).

5 Rule and response in nineteenth-century India

The best book on India's modern history is Judith M. Brown's *Modern India: the origins of an Asian democracy*, Oxford, 1985. Britain's approach to India in the decades before the Indian Mutiny is analysed in two important books: George D. Bearce, *British attitudes towards India, 1784–1858*, Westport, 1982 (first published 1961), and Eric Stokes, *The English Utilitarians and India*, Oxford, 1959. Despite its title, Thomas R. Metcalf's *The aftermath of revolt: India, 1857–1870*, New Delhi, 1990 (first published 1964) also contains much information on British policy towards India on the eve of the Mutiny, as well as a persuasive and fluently written exposition of Britain's response to the events of 1857.

Christopher Hibbert's *The great mutiny: India 1857*, London, 1978, is a readable narrative account. The civilian aspects of the 1857 rising are examined in Eric Stokes' *The peasant and the raj: studies in agrarian society and peasant rebellion in colonial India*, Cambridge, 1978. The introduction of Stokes' posthumous *The peasant armed: the Indian revolt of 1857*, Oxford, 1986, includes a useful survey of different historical approaches to the Mutiny.

Britain's burgeoning economic relationship with India is conveniently dealt with in Neil Charlesworth's *British rule and the Indian economy, 1800–1914*, London, 1982.

6 Imperialism and nationalism in India

A close analysis of the relationship between imperialism and nationalism is provided in two important articles: Anil Seal, 'Imperialism and nationalism in India', *Modern Asian Studies*, vol. 7 (1973), and John Gallagher and Anil Seal, 'Britain and India between the wars', *Modern Asian Studies*, vol. 15 (1981). D. A. Low's edited work, *The Congress and the raj: facets of the Indian struggle, 1917–47*, Oxford, 1977, contains a number of illuminating essays, most notably R. J. Moore's 'The crisis of freedom with unity: London's India policy, 1917–47'. The most comprehensive textbook covering the period of the nationalist challenge to Britain is Sumit Sarkar's *Modern India, 1885–1947*, Basingstoke, 1989.

The economic relationship between Britain and India from the late nineteenth century through to the transfer of power in 1947 is examined by B. R. Tomlinson in two articles and a book: 'India and the British Empire, 1880–1935', *Indian Economic and Social History Review*, vol. 12 (1975); 'India and the British Empire, 1935–47', *Indian Economic and Social History Review*, vol. 13 (1976); *The political economy of the raj, 1914–47*, London, 1979.

R. J. Moore's *Escape from empire: the Attlee government and the Indian problem*, Oxford, 1983, is a detailed analysis of British policy towards India in the last days of empire. The military considerations underpinning Britain's decision to leave India are covered by Hugh Tinker's article, 'The contraction of empire in Asia, 1945–8: the military dimension', *Journal of Imperial and Commonwealth History*, 16 (1988). A useful collection of essays is provided by C. H. Philips and M. D. Wainwright (eds.), *The partition of India: policies and perspectives, 1935–47*, London, 1970.

The role of M. A. Jinnah in the partition of India is given controversial, yet influential, treatment in Ayesha Jalal's *The sole spokesman: Jinnah, the Muslim League and the demand for Pakistan*, Cambridge, 1985. The best biography of Gandhi is Judith M. Brown's *Gandhi: prisoner of hope*, New Haven, 1989.

7 Britain's imperial century, 1815–1914

The starting point for an analysis of British policy in this period is Ronald Hyam's elegantly written *Britain's imperial century, 1815–1914*, 2nd edn, Basingstoke, 1993. P. J. Cain's concise survey, *Economic foundations of British overseas expansion, 1815–1914*, Basingstoke, 1980, represents a useful introduction to the vexed question of economics and empire. Andrew Porter's *European imperialism, 1869–1914*, Basingstoke, 1994, takes a thematic approach to the question of imperial expansion in the fifty years before the First World War.

By introducing the concept of 'informal empire', John Gallagher and Ronald Robinson's 'The imperialism of free trade', *Economic History Review*, vol. 6 (1953), transformed the way in which historians handled imperial questions. Their interpretation, however, has been subjected to close scrutiny: D. C. M. Platt, 'The imperialism of free trade: some reservations', *Economic History Review*, vol. 21 (1968); Platt, 'Further objections to an "imperialism of free trade", 1830–60', *Economic History Review*, vol. 26 (1973); Britten Dean, 'British informal empire: the case of China', *Journal of Commonwealth and Comparative Politics*, vol. 14 (1976); Martin Lynn, 'The "imperialism of free trade" and the case of West Africa, c. 1830–1870', *Journal of Imperial and Commonwealth History*, vol. 15 (1986).

An attempt to place the British economy back at the heart of the debate on imperial expansion has been made by P. J. Cain and A. G. Hopkins in a series of articles and books: 'Gentlemanly capitalism and British expansion overseas. I: The old colonial system, 1688–1850', *Economic History Review*, vol. 39 (1986); 'Gentlemanly capitalism and British expansion overseas. II: New imperialism, 1850–1945', *Economic History Review*, vol. 40 (1987); *British imperialism*, 2 vols., London, 1993.

M. E. Chamberlain's *The scramble for Africa*, Harlow, 1974, makes a brave attempt to demystify the European partition of Africa. Ronald Robinson and John Gallagher's Egyptocentric and strategic interpretation of the partition of Africa is offered in their influential *Africa and the Victorians: the official mind of imperialism*, 2nd edn, Basingstoke, 1981. Their analysis has been attacked in Hopkins' article 'The Victorians and Africa: a reconsideration of the occupation of Egypt, 1882', *Journal of African History*, vol. 27 (1986).

Lance E. Davis and Robert A. Huttenback question the value of empire in their *Mammon and the pursuit of empire: the political economy of British imperialism, 1860–1912*, Cambridge, 1986. This interpretation has found critics among the following: Andrew Porter, 'The balance sheet of empire, 1850–1914', *Historical Journal*, vol. 31 (1988); A. G. Hopkins, 'Accounting for the British Empire', *Journal of Imperial and Commonwealth History*, vol. 16 (1988); Avner Offer, 'The British Empire, 1870–1914: a waste of money?', *Economic History Review*, vol. 46 (1993).

Biographies of British statesmen who dominated the age include: Jasper Ridley, *Lord Palmerston*, London, 1970; Roy Jenkins, *Gladstone*, London, 1995; Robert Blake, *Disraeli*, London, 1966.

8 Challenges to imperial authority: South Africa and Ireland

The most even-handed and readable book on the tortured history of South Africa is Leonard Thompson's, *A history of South Africa*, New Haven, 1995. John S. Galbraith's *Reluctant empire: British policy on the South African frontier, 1834–1854*, Westport, 1963, is a classic study of Britain's relations with South Africa in the era of the Great Trek. J. D. Omer-Cooper's 'Colonial South Africa and its frontiers', in Monica Wilson and Leonard Thompson (eds.), *The Oxford history of South Africa*, vol. 1, Oxford, 1969, provides an overview of British policy in the first half of the nineteenth century. Thompson's 'Great Britain and the Afrikaner Republics, 1870–1899', in Wilson and Thompson, *Oxford history of South Africa*, vol. 2, Oxford, 1971, traces the breakdown of Anglo-Boer relations leading to war in 1899.

The South African War has spawned a vast literature. The best recent attempt to untangle this complex subject has been made by Iain R. Smith's *The origins of the South African War, 1899–1902*, London, 1996. A. N. Porter's *The origins of the South African War: Joseph Chamberlain and the diplomacy of imperialism, 1895–99*, Manchester, 1980 is also essential for an understanding of the thinking which underpinned the decision-making process in London. A reassessment of Britain's decision to grant responsible government to the Transvaal in 1906 is provided by Ronald Hyam's 'The myth of the "Magnanimous Gesture": the Liberal government, Smuts, and conciliation, 1906', in Ronald Hyam and Ged Martin (eds.), *Reappraisals in British imperial history*, London, 1975.

The most accessible book on Ireland's modern history is Michael Hughes' *Ireland divided: the roots of the modern Irish problem*, Cardiff, 1994. A more detailed, though more complex, treatment is provided by K. Theodore Hoppen's *Ireland since 1800: conflict and conformity*, London, 1989. The impact of problems in Ireland on the British scene is examined in D. G. Boyce's *The Irish question and British politics, 1868–1996*, 2nd edn, Basingstoke, 1996. A stimulating set of articles on Ireland's role within the British Empire is provided in Keith Jeffrey's edited work, *'An Irish empire?' Aspects of Ireland and the British Empire*, Manchester, 1996. Sympathy among Irish nationalists for the Boers is dealt with in Donal P. McCracken's *The Irish pro-Boers, 1877–1902*, Johannesburg, 1989.

9 The British Empire in the Middle East

Elizabeth Monroe's *Britain's moment in the Middle East, 1914–1971*, London, 1981 (first published 1963), while beginning to show its age, is still the best single volume on the rise and fall of British power in the Middle East.

Britain's unhappy relationship with Palestine is comprehensively covered in three books by Michael J. Cohen: *Palestine to Israel: from mandate to independence*, London, 1988; *Palestine: retreat from the mandate, 1936–45*, London, 1978; *Palestine and the great powers, 1945–1948*, Princeton, 1982.

Anglo-American relations in the Middle East are examined in two important books: William Roger Louis, *The British Empire in the Middle East, 1945–1951: Arab nationalism, the United States, and postwar imperialism*, Oxford, 1984; Ritchie Ovendale, *Britain, the United States, and the transfer of power in the Middle East, 1945–1962*, London, 1996.

David Carlton's *Britain and the Suez Crisis*, Oxford, 1988, is a concise and readable account. More detailed treatment is provided by Keith Kyle's *Suez*, New York, 1991. Two illuminating sets of documents on the Crisis have recently been produced: Scott Lucas (ed.), *Britain and Suez: the lion's last roar*, Manchester, 1996; Anthony Gorst and Lewis Johnman, *The Suez Crisis*, London, 1997.

10 End of empire: Africa

The most thorough general text is John D. Hargreaves' *Decolonization in Africa*, 2nd edn, London, 1996. For accounts of Britain's reassessment of policy from the late 1930s, see R. D. Pearce, *The turning point in Africa: British colonial policy, 1938–48*, London, 1982; John Flint, 'Planned decolonization and its failure in British Africa', *African Affairs*, vol. 82 (1983). Wartime attempts to refurbish Britain's imperial image are dealt with by Rosaleen Smyth's 'Britain's African colonies and British propaganda during the Second World War', *Journal of Imperial and Commonwealth History*, vol. 14 (1985).

The American role in British decolonisation is examined in two important contributions from William Roger Louis and Ronald Robinson: 'The United States and the liquidation of British Empire in Tropical Africa, 1941–1951', in Prosser Gifford and William Roger Louis (eds.), *The transfer of power in Africa: decolonization, 1940–1960*, New Haven, 1982; 'The imperialism of decolonization', *Journal of Imperial and Commonwealth History*, vol. 22 (1994).

Post-war Labour policy towards Africa is surveyed in the following: John W. Cell, 'On the eve of decolonization: the Colonial Office's plans for the transfer of power in Africa, 1947', *Journal of Imperial and Commonwealth History*, vol. 8 (1980); Ronald Hyam, 'Africa and the Labour government, 1945–51', *Journal of Imperial and Commonwealth History*, vol. 16 (1988); Ronald Robinson, 'Sir Andrew Cohen: pro-consul of African nationalism', in L. H. Gann and P. Duignan (eds.), *African pro-consuls*, Stanford, 1978.

Conservative policy towards Africa is scrutinised in the following: Dan Horowitz, 'Attitudes of British Conservatives towards decolonization in Africa', *African Affairs*, vol. 69 (1970); David Goldsworthy, 'Conservatives and decolonization: a note on the interpretation of Dan Horowitz', *African Affairs*, vol. 69 (1970); Ritchie Ovendale, 'Macmillan and the winds of change in Africa, 1957–1960', *Historical Journal*, vol. 38 (1995).

The unhappy history of the Central African Federation is traced in two important articles: Ronald Hyam, 'The geopolitical origins of the Central African Federation: Britain, Rhodesia and South Africa, 1948–1953', *Historical Journal*, vol. 30 (1987); Prosser Gifford, 'Misconceived dominion: the creation and disintegration of federation in British Central Africa', in Prosser Gifford and William Roger Louis (eds.), *The transfer of power in Africa: decolonization, 1940–1960*, New Haven, 1982.

Index

Index